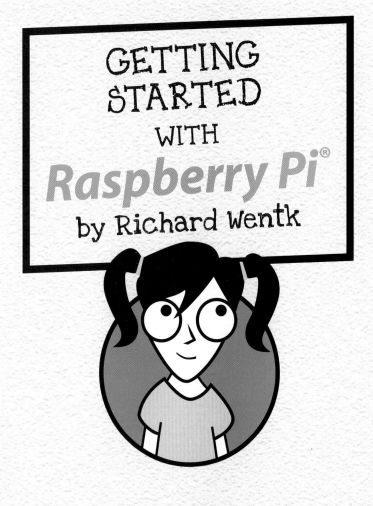

GETTING STARTED WITH Raspberry Pi®

by Richard Wentk

WILEY

GETTING STARTED WITH RASPBERRY PI®

Published by
John Wiley & Sons, Inc.
111 River Street
Hoboken, NJ 07030-5774

www.wiley.com

CONTENTS

INTRODUCTION ABOUT RASPBERRY PI

SO YOU WANT TO BUY A RASPBERRY PI! Do you want to know more about how computers work? Do you want to look inside them to find out what really happens when you click a mouse, press a key on a keyboard, click a link on a website, or launch an app?

This book is for you! It introduces you to the world of the tiny Raspberry Pi computer, which is perfect for learning how computers work.

Unlike big, expensive computers, the Pi is designed to be hands-on. You can get right inside it and make it do tricks that are much harder to do on a PC or a Mac — never mind an Android tablet or an iPad.

ABOUT THIS BOOK

The good news is that in some ways, the Pi is very easy to use. But it wouldn't be fair to pretend that it's always simple.

In other ways, it can be harder to manage than a Mac or a PC. Because it's hands-on, you sometimes have to think harder about what you're doing.

But the Pi is really good for learning how computers work on the inside and for building simple software and hardware projects. It's also good for learning more about learning, which means finding out how to do your own research on the Internet.

This book is your guide to the fascinating world waiting for you inside your Pi. You can use it to learn:

» Why the Raspberry Pi is special

» What parts you need to add to a Pi to make it work and how much they cost

» Where to find the latest free software for your Pi

» How to power up and power down a Pi

» How to start using the Linux operating system

» What you can do with Scratch, a simple programming system

» Why the Sonic Pi music programming system is a ton of fun

» How to write code and draw pictures using the popular Python language

» How you can use Python to control your character in the Pi version of Minecraft

ABOUT YOU

Getting Started with Raspberry Pi makes some guesses about what you know already.

» You don't need to know anything about code or be a computer genius. But you need some basic computer skills, like the ones on this list:

1 You can use a Mac or a PC or maybe even a Linux computer.

2 You're comfortable with a mouse and keyboard, and you can find your way around your computer's desktop.

3 You're not scared of plugging together computer parts to add extras.

4 You're fine with using Google or some other search engine to look up things on the Internet.

» You have a little (but not much) cash to spare. Fifty dollars will cover most of what you need, and $100 will cover everything easily.

» You know some basic math, and you're not too scared of adding, subtracting, multiplying, and dividing. (You don't have to be brilliant at doing them in your head. That's what computers are for!)

ICONS USED IN THIS BOOK

Some of the pages of this book have little round pictures at the sides. Here's what they mean:

 Tips make your life easier. You'll want to take advantage of them.

 When you see this icon, pay special attention, because it points out information you don't want to forget.

 This text warns you of things that can go wrong . . . so be careful!

WHERE TO GO FROM HERE

You can read this book in any order that makes sense to you. You can flip through it to find new ideas or go through it in order.

I recommend you work through at least the first couple of projects in order. If you're new to the Raspberry Pi, those early projects have everything you need to get started.

The rest is up to you. Good luck — and don't forget to have fun and do cool things!

BEFORE YOU CAN MAKE A PI, YOU NEED TO BUY SOME PI PARTS. Unlike a Mac or PC, you can pick and choose between many possible options. Or you can be clever: To save time, you can buy a kit with everything you need.

UNDERSTANDING THE PI SYSTEM

When you buy a PC or a Mac, you get a carful of boxes and extras, and most of the time you get everything you need.

When you buy a Pi, you get a tiny slab of electronics the size of a credit card.

The slab is called a *board* because it's flat like a board. So the main part of the Pi is sometimes called the *Pi board*.

Case? No. Keyboard? Uh uh. Mouse? Not included.

So before you can use your Pi, you have to add a lot of extras. Most homes have the right kind of extras lying around in cupboards, attics, and dens, collecting dust, so you can probably find the right parts you need at home.

But you'll still have to buy some parts — including the Pi itself.

This project is about collecting parts. Don't plug them all together yet! It's especially important you don't try to power up your Pi until you've collected the parts, connected them all together, and followed the instructions in the next project. You can break something if you rush in, so don't. Yet.

PICKING A PI MODEL

The Pi has been around for a while now, so there's more than one kind of Pi. You'll see Model As and Model Bs and Pi Zeroes, and all kinds of other things.

Keep it simple. You want a *Raspberry Pi Model 2*. It's the latest, fastest, and best Pi ever. It's very cheap, and it does everything you want.

Technically, the full name is the Model 2 B+. But you can ignore the B+ on the end, because usually it's just called a Pi 2.

Don't buy anything that isn't a Pi 2. Older Pi models aren't as good as the 2. And you can ignore the Pi Zero. It's really, really cheap, but it doesn't do half the things that a Pi 2 does, and this book won't mention it again, even though it's quite cool, in a tiny way.

UNDERSTANDING MUST-HAVE EXTRAS

Must-have extras aren't optional. Your Pi system has to include them, or you can't use it.

Here's a list:

- » USB keyboard
- » USB mouse

» Monitor

» Monitor cable

» Memory card

» Power supply

» Long network cable

» Space to set up

PICKING A MOUSE AND KEYBOARD

Many homes have an old mouse and keyboard gathering dust. The make and model don't matter, as long as both items have a USB cable — that's the cable that looks like a long thin rectangular slot and plugs into another long thin slot, usually the wrong way around because no one ever plugs it in right the first time.

Bluetooth wireless keyboards won't work, so you can't use an Android/iPad keyboard or one of those thin and clicky Apple keyboards that doesn't have a cable coming out the back.

You can use a wireless mouse and/or keyboard as long as they have a USB dongle — a tiny USB plug that picks up the mouse and/or keyboard by radio magic. Logitech is a good name to look for, but most wireless brands should work.

PICKING A MONITOR

Almost any modern-ish LCD monitor will do. The Pi doesn't have brilliant graphics, so the monitor doesn't have to be expensive.

If you don't care about elbowing the rest of the family out of the way while they're watching their favorite shows, you can probably use the family TV. A monitor of your own is better and will keep everyone else sweet.

PICKING A MONITOR CABLE

The Pi has a special socket for a monitor cable. It's called an HDMI socket, and it's long, thin, and flat — even longer and thinner than a USB socket.

Your monitor cable should have an HDMI plug at one end. The other end depends on the monitor. If you're lucky, your monitor also has an HDMI socket. If so, you can use a plain HDMI-to-HDMI lead with exactly the same plug at each end. (You can look online or ask at a store for one.) Job done.

If you're less lucky, it depends. If your monitor has a DVI socket (search online for a picture), you need to buy a DVI-to-HDMI adaptor cable.

If it has a VGA connector (search online again), you need to buy an adaptor *and* a cable and hope they work, because sometimes they don't. (Look for an HDMI-to-VGA Male-to-Female Adaptor.)

If you — or your parents — can afford it, it's often better to get a cheap new monitor with an HDMI socket rather than fool around with adaptors. You can find made-for-Pi HDMI monitors from around $70 online. You can also pick up cheap used HDMI monitors on eBay, Craigslist, and Amazon. New, they cost around $130, which may be more than you want to pay.

If you don't already have the right cable in the house, Amazon and eBay are the cheapest places to look. You can also buy them in local stores of all kinds, but they can be insanely expensive. Some stores charge more for an HDMI cable than for a Raspberry Pi!

PICKING A MEMORY CARD

The Pi doesn't have a disk drive. Instead, it uses a tiny memory card. The one you want is a micro SD card with more than 4GB of space.

Micro SD cards are tiny and easy to lose, so they often come with an SD card adaptor, which isn't quite so tiny, but is still easy to lose. You don't need one for the Pi, but it can be a good thing to have (if you don't lose it).

You can buy a blank card, but there's a better option: Buy a card with the Pi software preloaded on it. The software is called NOOBS, and you can buy preloaded cards from a lot of places online. Search for NOOBS to see a list of shops.

Make sure you get the latest, freshest version of NOOBS. This book was written for version 1.5. Check the Raspberry Pi Foundation site at www.raspberrypi.org/downloads/noobs to see the latest version number and then check that the number is the same when you buy your card.

It's not hard to put NOOBS onto a blank card. But it's a long and boooooring process, and it needs special card-formatting software that you have to download and install on a Mac or PC. And a card reader. You can find instructions online if you want them, but trust me — it's a lot of time and effort to save a couple of bucks.

PICKING A POWER SUPPLY

The Pi doesn't have a power switch or a built-in cable to the power socket on the wall.

Instead, it uses a blob of plastic and electronics sometimes called a *wall wart*. It plugs into the wall, and you have to connect it to the Pi using a special cable — just like a phone or tablet charger.

The power socket on the Pi is *tiny*. It's called a micro USB plug.

Some power supplies have the right cable attached. They're often labeled Raspberry Pi power supplies. If you get one, you should be fine.

Others have one or more big familiar USB sockets. These power supplies are often sold as chargers for phones and tablets, but you can use them with a Pi as long as you get a special cable with a standard USB plug at one end and one of those micro USB type B plugs at the other for the Pi.

Look on Amazon or eBay, as usual. The cable you want is called a USB 2.0 A-Male to 2.0 B-Micro cable. You can get any length up to 3 feet or so.

The charger and cable version is easier to plug and unplug, which is a good thing. Remember, the Pi doesn't have a power switch! Sometimes you have to start it by turning the power off and on again by pulling the plug out and pushing it back. The micro USB socket can break if you do this too often, so it's better to do it at the big standard USB end.

Got all that? You're not done yet! You need to pick a power supply labeled with 2A or more. If it's 1A or 1.5A, that's not enough. 2.2A is fine. So are 2.5A and 4.8A. You get the idea.

The *A* is short for Amps. 2A and 2 Amps are the same.

PICKING A NETWORK CABLE

Your Pi needs an Internet connection. The best way to make one is to buy a Cat 6 Ethernet cable. The cable has to be long enough to plug into the family modem/router/Internet box.

This can be a problem if you want to work in your bedroom and the Internet connection is downstairs. Get a flat cable if you can — they're more expensive, but much better — and make sure that it's long enough.

Ethernet isn't another name for Internet. It's a special kind of cable often used for connecting computers to the Internet. As usual, you can find out more by searching for Ethernet cable online.

Nail it down, or ask someone else to nail it down for you, to make sure that no one trips over it. Loose cables all over a house are very bad!

What about WiFi? WiFi is great when it works. No cables! But it doesn't always work. A cable is better if you can make it work in your house. If you really can't, you can find out more about WiFi in the next section.

Your Pi doesn't need Internet all the time. Some features won't work without it, but you don't need it for most of the projects in this book. So if a connection is a problem, you can set up your Pi by the Internet box, get everything working, and then unplug it and move it somewhere else. This isn't as handy as having a connection all the time, but it will get you started.

FINDING SPACE

You need enough space for a monitor, mouse, and keyboard. This may be more space than you expect, especially if you become a Pi expert and start building electronic projects around it. So grab the biggest space you can find.

Use a desk or table if you can. If you can't find a desk, maybe you can set up on the floor. It won't be as comfortable as a desk, but it will do to get started, as long as you get a desk soon and remember not to step on the Pi by accident.

Some people like to use a kitchen table for computer experiments. Kitchen tables are big and flat, but kitchens are used for cooking and eating, so you probably won't be able to keep your Pi set up. If you really can't find anywhere else in the house, check with the grown-ups to see whether it's okay to use the kitchen before setting up.

PICKING NICE-TO-HAVE EXTRAS

You can make your Pi work as long as you have all the things I describe in the preceding sections. But it can be nice to add more to your Pi. Here are a few extras you'll see online.

ADDING A CASE

You don't really need a case, but a good one will help protect your Pi from falling objects, fat fingers, and annoying brothers or sisters.

Search the web for Raspberry Pi case to see a very long list of cases. Pick one that looks good. They all do more or less the same thing. A/B, A+/B+, and Pi 2 cases are different, so make sure that you get the right one. The photo shows a Pi inside a typical case.

If you live somewhere hot, get a case with air holes to help keep your Pi cool and ventilated.

If you don't use a case, put your Pi on something that doesn't conduct electricity. Thick paper, cardboard, wood, plastic, glass, and ceramics (plates and such) are all fine.

Baking trays, metal foil, knives, forks, and spoons, silver plates, and gold bars are all bad because they can connect things that shouldn't be connected, which is called making a *short circuit*.

If you're lucky, a short circuit will stop your Pi until you restart it. If you're not, it will kill your Pi dead forever and burn down the house. (Although if you have gold bars to spare, you can always buy another Pi. Or ten. And a house.)

Pi boards don't like static electricity. When you pick up a Pi board, hold it by the sides or by a USB or network socket. Don't prod the electronics with your fingers. Don't keep your Pi on the carpet or drag it over carpet. (Also, don't put it in the microwave and turn the power on, dissolve it in acid, or feed it to sharks. But you knew that anyway, huh?)

If you don't want to spend money on a case, you can print a case using cardboard! See www.raspberrypi.org/the-punnet-a-card-case-for-you-to-print-for-free.

ADDING WIFI

The Pi isn't great at WiFi. It's not easy to set it up, and sometimes it just doesn't work. Or it works for a while and then stops for no reason.

This is partly because the Pi doesn't have WiFi built in. It was left out to save money. If you want WiFi, you have to add a *WiFi dongle,* which is a small plastic thingy that plugs into one of the USB sockets.

There are a lot of WiFi dongles you can use, and they're all slightly different. WiFi also uses a lot of power, and sometimes the Pi doesn't like this.

If you want a WiFi dongle, you'll get the best results from the official Pi dongle you can buy from various Pi suppliers. Other dongles are hit and miss. You may get lucky and find one that works — or maybe not.

ADDING A CAMERA

A camera is a popular Pi extra. Most USB webcams work just fine with the Pi, but very old or very cheap webcams (less than $10) may not.

There is an official Pi Camera Module, which is a tiny electronic board with an even tinier camera that works better than you expect it to.

The Pi comes with ready-made software for the camera, so unlike a webcam, you don't have to write your own.

The camera is quite delicate. If you use it a lot, you'll want to put your Pi and the camera inside a special camera-friendly case. Search the web for Pi camera case for the latest options.

The official Pi camera comes in two types: standard and noIR, which is short for no infrared filter. You can use the noIR camera to make spooky ghostcam photos and videos using invisible infrared light. Most people buy the standard model. If you want to make a wildlife camera or hunt ghosts, get the noIR version.

ADDING LOUDSPEAKERS AND HEADPHONES

The Pi has a standard audio jack socket, like the ones on many mobile phones and MP3 players. You can plug a pair of speakers or headphones into the socket. If the Pi makes some noise, you'll hear it.

You'll need some way to listen to your Pi for the Sonic Pi project in this book. The rest of the time, noise is optional.

Because the Pi doesn't have built-in Bluetooth, it won't work with a Bluetooth speaker. It also doesn't work with Apple or Android phone docks.

ADDING HATS

The Pi can wear many hats. In Pi Land, a HAT isn't something you wear on your head.

In fact, you can wear Pi HATS on your head. But you'll look very silly, so it's best not to.

HATS are add-on electronic boards that do all kinds of things. They plug into the Pi, and the best ones don't wobble much.

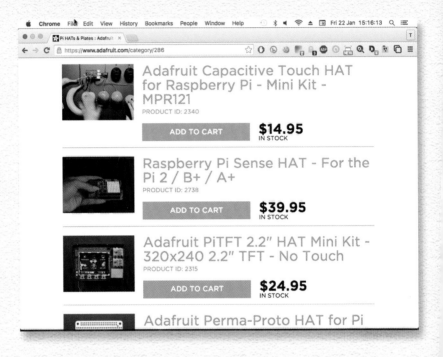

You can buy HATS that

» Add a small touch-sensitive display

» Display a grid of colored lights

» Measure temperature and dampness (humidity)

» Sense where your fingers are above the hat

» Play musical notes on a tiny keyboard

» Work out where you are in the world

» Control a motor

» Make it easier to plug together simple electronic circuits

» Play very high quality sound

There are also very expensive, very complicated hats that can fly a drone!

This book is a get-you-started book and not a complete-guide-to-everything-Pi book, so there isn't room here to get into the full details of adding and using HATS.

You need to know more about Pi basics first. But when you do, you can go exploring to see just what amazing extras you can add.

COLLECTING PARTS THE LAZY WAY: STARTER KITS

The smart way to buy a Pi system is to buy a Pi starter kit from a Pi shop. The right Pi kit will have everything you need, except a monitor and (usually) a monitor cable. Search online for Raspberry Pi starter kit to find the latest deals.

But be careful! Not all starter kits are the same.

PICKING THE RIGHT PI

Make sure that you get a kit with a Pi 2, and not an older model, such as a Model B+. (Does it say Pi 2 anywhere in the description? If so, you should be fine.)

DON'T BUY ELECTRONICS KITS

Some shops sell kits of electronic parts for Pi projects. You may want one later, but you can't start with one! Make sure that your kit includes at least a power supply and memory card with NOOBS with the Pi 2. If it includes a mouse and keyboard, too, that saves you from buying them or finding them.

But if the kit only has electronic parts and no power supply or memory card, that's not what you want.

CHECKING WHAT YOU'VE GOT

To save money, raid the family computer spares box and see what you find. You'll often discover old mice and keyboards, cables, and perhaps even an old monitor.

If your family doesn't have one, you can try asking uncles and aunts. Or you can get together with your friends to see what they've got!

Table 1-1 is a list of Pi parts. You can check off items as you find them or buy them.

TABLE 1-1   A HANDY PI CHECKLIST

Extra	Do I Need One?	Can I Find a Spare One?	Do I Need to Buy One?
Monitor	Must have		
USB keyboard	Must have		
USB mouse	Must have		
2A power supply	Must have		
Special power cable	Depends on the power supply		
4GB NOOBS card	Must have		
Ethernet cable	Must have		
WiFi dongle	Only if you can't use an Ethernet cable		
HDMI-to-HDMI cable	Depends on monitor		
HDMI-to-DVI cable	Depends on monitor		
Case	Nice to have		
Speakers or headphones	Needed for Project 4		

PROJECT 2 POWER ON YOUR PI

GETTING YOUR PI UP AND RUNNING ISN'T HARD WHEN YOU HAVE ALL THE PARTS YOU NEED. You just need to plug everything together, fit the memory card, turn on the power, click a few boxes, and wait. . . .

FINDING AND RECOGNIZING PARTS

You should really work through Project 1 now if you haven't already. Otherwise, you won't have the parts you need, and you won't know what they're called!

This project may seem like a lot of plugging things into other things, and you may worry you're doing it wrong.

Worry not: You can't plug anything into the wrong hole on the Pi because it won't fit! If you're forcing something, you're doing it wrong.

If you're still not sure about the names of things, search for pictures and examples online. Looking things up online is so useful for Pi projects that it should be the first thing you try.

SETTING UP YOUR PI SYSTEM

Did you find a good place for your Pi in the previous project? If you didn't, think about where your Pi can go. It's better to set up your Pi once and leave it set up. But if you don't have space, it's okay to set it up when you want to play with it and put it away when you're done.

You may think your Pi isn't very big, so it's easy to find space for it. But you need space for the keyboard, mouse, and monitor, too.

If you already have a Mac or PC, you can maybe keep the space you use already and add the Pi to it. If not, find some space now and make sure that it's big enough.

You may also need to find a power strip with lots of sockets. Your Pi needs at least two sockets — one for the monitor and one for the Pi. If you start building projects around it, you may need more power. Any strip will do. It doesn't have to be a fancy expensive professional super-strip that can protect your house from lightning strikes.

SETTING UP DESKS AND CHAIRS

If you spend a lot of time at a computer, you can grow up hunched and pale, which is bad, so you need to make sure that your chair is comfortable.

If your back or neck hurts after a while, you need to find a chair that's either higher or lower, depending on your height. Cushions to sit on can help, too.

MAKING THE CONNECTIONS

The Pi is easy to set up. You can't plug it together in the wrong way, because all the plugs and sockets are different. You can't force plugs into holes they don't fit into — not unless they're so stiff you need a hammer, which is usually a clue you're doing something wrong.

PLUGGING IN THE POWER

Start by plugging the Pi power supply and monitor into a power strip or two wall sockets if you don't have a power strip. You can power up the monitor now, but don't power up the Pi yet!

CONNECTING THE PI PARTS

To make connecting the Pi parts easy, here's a list of steps. It's best to do them in order.

1 **Plug the USB plug on the keyboard into a USB socket on the Pi board.**

It doesn't matter which one you use.

2 Plug the mouse into another USB socket.

3 Plug the Ethernet (network) cable into your home broadband box or router.

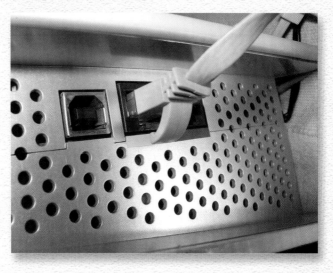

On most routers, all the sockets do the same thing. If you plug in a network cable, everything just works. On a few routers, one or two of the sockets may not be like the others. If you see different colors around the sockets, like the photo shows, try asking for help. Or — better — look online to see how to make your router work.

4 Plug the other end of the network cable into the biggest socket on the Pi.

5 Plug the big flat HDMI cable into the Pi.

6 Plug the other end of the HDMI cable into your monitor.

If you have an HDMI-to-HDMI cable, look for a thin, flat socket. If you have an HDMI-to-DVI cable, look online to see what a DVI socket looks like and plug the DVI end into the monitor.

1 Plug the NOOBS card into the card slot on the Pi.

The metal pins face up, and the card slot is under the Pi. (The photo shows the Pi and the card from underneath, just to confuse you.)

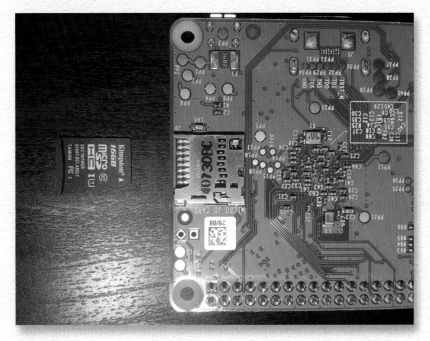

Make sure that the card clicks into place with a quiet snick. To take out the card, push it until it un-snicks. Then plug it back in again.

You don't usually need to remove the card after you plug it in. You especially shouldn't ever — never, not even once for a dare — take out the card with the power on. You'll probably break the Pi and the card, which will make everyone sad. Boo!

GETTING READY TO TURN ON THE PI

Your Pi should look something like the photo, with a bare board, or possibly a bare board inside a plastic case, surrounded by connections.

The power connection goes last. It's at the top right of the photo — the micro USB power cable.

Double-check that everything is where it should be. Then when you're ready, plug the cable into the tiny power socket.

Don't plug in any unusual extras: no HATS, no webcams, no PiCams, nothing. Keep it simple. You can add extras later when you know the Pi is working.

You can see the HDMI cable at the top of the photo. It's the big, black, plastic blob plugged into the metal thing on the Pi board.

It has HDMI on it, which is a handy clue.

The power socket is quite stiff. It's designed to hold the cable so that you can't pull it out by accident. You may have to push and jiggle it a bit to make it go in. But before you push and jiggle too much, make sure that you have the cable the right way up. If the cable doesn't move at all when you push, turn the cable over.

When you get around to powering down the Pi — don't do it yet — leave the micro USB socket connected and pull the power supply out of the power strip. The power socket on the board isn't very strong, and if you keep plugging and unplugging it, it may break.

LIGHTS! CAMERA! ACTION!

If you made all the right connections, the Pi will spark — hopefully, not literally — into life when you apply the power.

Powering up a computer is sometimes called *booting* it. It's short for bootstrapping, supposedly because the computer has to pull itself up by its bootstraps before it can do anything. Except computers don't have boots. And not many boots have straps. And even if boots did have straps, no one has ever pulled himself up by them. So none of this makes any sense. But still. That's what it's called.

SETTING UP THE PI

Your Pi does nothing out of the box. Before you can use it, you have to do some setting up. The NOOBS card tries to make this as easy as it can be.

If your NOOBS card is working and the Pi is working, the Pi shows you a big box full of strange words that you don't understand, with checkboxes next to them.

Find the checkbox marked Raspbian — it's in the highlighted area at the top of the list — and click it with the mouse. If you do this right, a small cross appears in the box.

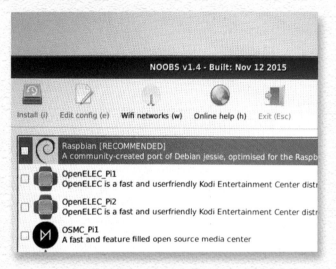

At the bottom of the screen, find the box that says Language and Keyboard. Click the Language menu with the mouse to select English UK or English US, depending where you live.

Click the Keyboard menu with the mouse and select a matching keyboard — so gb for the UK and us for the United States.

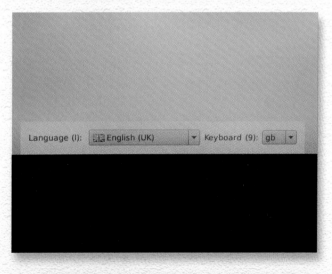

You might think that keyboards are all the same. They're not. The letters are all in the same places, but some shapes like the @ used in email addresses can be in different places. If you skip this step, your Pi may not always show the shapes you type. There is a way to fix this, but it's not simple, so it's better to get it right.

Now go back to the top left of the screen and click the button labeled Install. Your Pi should now start doing stuff. The stuff takes a while. While you're waiting, read the explanation of what you just did in the sidebar "Raspbian, Linux, and the Pi."

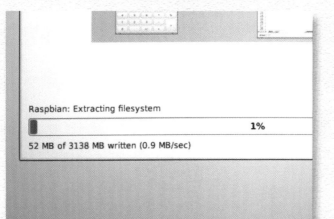

RASPBIAN, LINUX, AND THE PI

All computers have built-in software that keeps the computer working and tries to make sense of your mouse clicks and your typing.

(Continued)

(Continued)

On a Mac, the operating system is called OS X. On a PC, it's called Windows. On the Pi, it's called Linux.

Linux isn't like OS X or Windows.

It's free. You never pay for Linux. And if you're very good at computers, you can change the insides of Linux to make it work how you want. You can't do that with OS X and Windows because the people who make them don't let you.

Because it's easy to change and people enjoy playing with it, Linux comes in lots of different versions. Some versions do one job, like managing and playing a music and video collection. Others are for general computing.

When you boot NOOBS, it installs a version of Linux with a weird name: Raspbian. The name comes from a version of Linux called Debian, which is very popular. Raspbian is really just Debian with a few changes to make it work well on the Pi.

The current version is called Jessie — for no good reason. (The previous version was called Wheezy, which makes even less sense. No one knows what the next version will be called. Grumpy? Sneezy? Dopey? Your guess is as good as anyone's.)

The Pi is not a fast computer, so installing Linux takes a while. While you're waiting, you can see a progress bar, which gives you some idea how much longer you have to wait. You can also read a little about Raspbian and Linux in the splash screens above the progress bar.

BOOTING INTO RASPBIAN

When NOOBS is done — this can take a long time — the Pi eventually loads Raspbian, and it starts working. This is called *booting into Raspbian.*

The first thing that happens is that the monitor fills with computer gibberish, which scrolls by very fast. If you're a Linux expert, the gibberish tells you what Linux is doing as it boots.

```
[    3.215550] usb 1-1.1: New USB device strings: Mfr=0, Product=0, SerialNumber=0
[    3.244001] smsc95xx v1.0.4
[    3.317090] smsc95xx 1-1.1:1.0 eth0: register 'smsc95xx' at usb-bcm2708_usb-1.1, smsc95xx USB 2.0 E
thernet, b8:27:eb:30:b2:e9
[    3.422153] usb 1-1.4: new low-speed USB device number 4 using dwc_otg
[    3.562456] usb 1-1.4: New USB device found, idVendor=062a, idProduct=0201
[    3.586245] usb 1-1.4: New USB device strings: Mfr=0, Product=1, SerialNumber=0
[    3.611171] usb 1-1.4: Product: USB-compliant keyboard
[    3.650374] input: USB-compliant keyboard as /devices/platform/bcm2708_usb/usb1/1-1/1-1.4/1-1.4:1.0
/input/input0
[    3.682519] hid-generic 0003:062A:0201.0001: input,hidraw0: USB HID v1.10 Keyboard [USB-compliant k
eyboard] on usb-bcm2708_usb-1.4/input0
[    3.756437] input: USB-compliant keyboard as /devices/platform/bcm2708_usb/usb1/1-1/1-1.4/1-1.4:1.1
/input/input1
[    3.792959] hid-generic 0003:062A:0201.0002: input,hiddev0,hidraw1: USB HID v1.10 Mouse [USB-compli
ant keyboard] on usb-bcm2708_usb-1.4/input1
[    3.922118] usb 1-1.5: new low-speed USB device number 5 using dwc_otg
[    4.057163] usb 1-1.5: New USB device found, idVendor=04f2, idProduct=0939
[    4.079687] usb 1-1.5: New USB device strings: Mfr=0, Product=2, SerialNumber=0
[    4.093412] usb 1-1.5: Product: USB Optical Mouse
[    4.132070] input: USB Optical Mouse as /devices/platform/bcm2708_usb/usb1/1-1/1-1.5/1-1.5:1.0/inpu
t/input2
[    4.162522] hid-generic 0003:04F2:0939.0003: input,hidraw2: USB HID v1.11 Mouse [USB Optical Mouse]
on usb-bcm2708_usb-1.5/input0
[    4.368336] udevd[158]: starting version 175
[   13.041386] EXT4-fs (mmcblk0p7): re-mounted. Opts: (null)
[   13.607852] EXT4-fs (mmcblk0p7): re-mounted. Opts: (null)
[   22.719491] smsc95xx 1-1.1:1.0 eth0: hardware isn't capable of remote wakeup
[   24.303158] smsc95xx 1-1.1:1.0 eth0: link up, 100Mbps, full-duplex, lpa 0xCDE1
[   30.003546] Adding 102396k swap on /var/swap.  Priority:-1 extents:1 across:102396k SSFS
[   93.424727] EXT4-fs (mmcblk0p3): mounted filesystem with ordered data mode. Opts: (null)
[   95.178836] EXT4-fs (mmcblk0p5): mounted filesystem with ordered data mode. Opts: (null)

The programs included with the Debian GNU/Linux system are free software;
the exact distribution terms for each program are described in the
individual files in /usr/share/doc/*/copyright.

Debian GNU/Linux comes with ABSOLUTELY NO WARRANTY, to the extent
permitted by applicable law.

pi@raspberrypi ~ $ []
```

If you're not a Linux expert, you can ignore it because it's not all that interesting.

Are we done yet? No! When the letters disappear, you have to wait . . . and wait . . . and wait some more, while Raspbian does some more setting up of its own.

Because the screen goes blank, you may worry that your Pi has died. It hasn't. On the current version of Raspbian, this extra setup takes a good long while. While it's happening, your Pi sits there with a mouse cursor on the screen.

Luckily, the setup only happens the first time you use Raspbian. When you start up your Pi again, it doesn't take nearly as long (but it may be longer than you want).

There's a tiny yellow light on one corner of the Pi board. If this light is flickering, your Pi is thinking. If it goes out for a long time and only the red light is left, something has gone wrong.

Do not panic. Do not unplug the Pi while you wait — for at least half an hour. If nothing at all is happening by the end, try turning the power off and on again. If that doesn't help, try another NOOBS card. If that still doesn't help, try another NOOBS card and another Pi.

LOOKING AT THE DESKTOP

When Raspbian finishes getting ready, the Pi boots into the desktop.

The Pi desktop is a lot like a traditional Windows or OS X desktop. There's a wastebasket for trash. There's a menu bar that does the usual menu bar things when you click on it. There's a collection of icons. And there's a giant Raspberry Pi logo.

The Pi logo is the desktop wallpaper. It doesn't do anything when you click on it. It would be cool if it did — maybe by playing a raspberry sound. Sadly, no.

This book is a brief introduction to the Pi, and not a complete course in Pi-ology. So here's a short summary of the desktop items. There's more about some of the items in later projects.

From left to right at the top left:

» Click the **Menu button** to see a menu of software that's already installed for you.

» Click the **Epiphany web browser** to launch a web browser. This browser is very slow, but sometimes it's useful for looking things up.

» Use the **File Manager** to explore the file system, copy files, rename them, and so on.

» The **Terminal** opens up the insides of Linux for expert users. Use it to type powerful magic text commands that only Linux wizards know.

» **Mathematica** and **Wolfram** are two applications for math geeks. They're very clever and sometimes useful, especially if you want to cheat at math homework. But they're really for older Pi users.

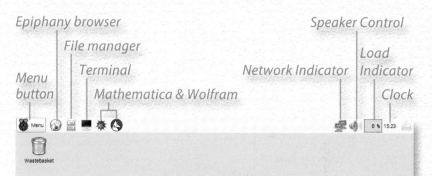

Epiphany browser

File manager

Menu button   Terminal   Mathematica & Wolfram

Network Indicator   Speaker Control   Load Indicator   Clock

And then from left to right, at the top right:

» The **network indicator** flashes when information comes into or flows out of the Pi.

» Use the **speaker control** to set the volume of headphones and speakers.

» The Pi doesn't have a busy mouse cursor. Instead, it has the **Load Indicator,** a box with a graph showing how busy the Pi is and a percentage. 0% means relaxed and waiting; 100% means the Pi is as busy as it can be.

» Click the **Clock** to show a calendar.

» Don't click **Disk Eject** while the Pi is running because the Pi won't be able to find its memory card anymore.

There's also a programming menu. When you click the Menu button, you see quite a few options to explore. In the rest of this book, you're going to play with a few of the items in the Programming menu: Scratch, Sonic Pi, and Python.

THE LINUX COMMAND LINE

Linux is a hands-on operating system. The best way to get hands-on with it is to use the Terminal application to type text commands.

If you're used to using a mouse, typing text commands feels weird. It's like dealing with an unusual, stupid, and literal robot that has no idea what you mean and has to be told exactly what to do.

When you type a command, it has to be perfect. You can't make a mistake. All the words, letters, and numbers have to be in the right place.

If they're not, Linux won't understand what you want. Worse, sometimes the command will do something, but it may not be what you want. (For example, you can *delete all the files* on your Pi with a short one-line command. There is never a reason why you would want to do this, but Linux doesn't try to stop you.)

This makes commands a pain. But they also have an upside. You can chain commands together to make little mini-programs that do useful things.

This makes Linux incredibly powerful. You can do things like move all your music or video files onto a single disk or send yourself an email when something interesting happens on website you like reading.

(Continued)

(Continued)

Command-line programming is not for beginners, and it's a bit too hard for a simple get-started book like this one. It takes a while to understand what you can do and even longer to understand how to do it.

A lot of commands are more like magic words. You can't work them out for yourself, no matter how clever you are. You need someone to tell you what to type, or you need to look it up online.

If you want to find out more, there's plenty to explore online. Search for Linux command line. If you want to experiment, launch the Terminal application and start typing.

You'll probably get very frustrated to start with, and then — maybe, eventually — you'll suddenly think "Wow! This is amazing! I had no idea you could do this!"

PROJECT 3 START SCRATCH FROM SCRATCH

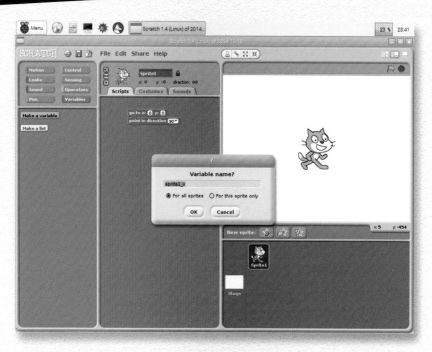

YOU CAN USE YOUR PI TO MAKE GAMES AND PLAY WITH REAL CODE. There's more about code and custom software in Project 5. This project is about a simple way to get started with coding. It's called Scratch, and it's a lot of fun.

Scratch was made for kids, but adults can use it, too. It's a really good way to get started with coding before moving to Python and other languages. And it's free!

UNDERSTANDING SCRATCH

Scratch is the simplest way ever to make your own software by creating computer code.

Usually when you write code, you type words that look a bit — but not much — like English. With Scratch, you don't have to type anything. You get a big (virtual) box of blocks and a stage where things happen. Each block does something different.

The stage has characters called *sprites*. Some blocks move a sprite. Other blocks turn a sprite or make it change color. Some blocks check whether a sprite is touching another sprite or the sides of the stage.

You can make sprites show talk bubbles or think bubbles, grow or shrink, change color, and do all kinds of other tricks.

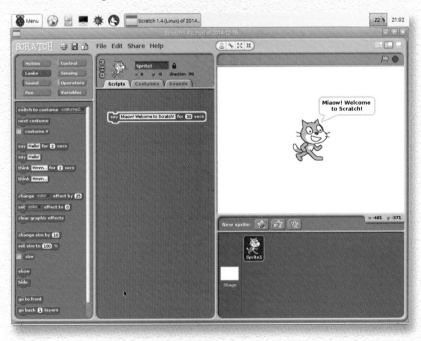

You don't have to use Scratch on your Pi. The scratch website at scratch.mit.edu includes a version of Scratch that runs in a web browser. The Pi version is less polished than the web version. But you probably have the Pi all to yourself, so you won't have to wait to use the family computer to use Scratch.

CONNECTING BLOCKS AND MAKING SCRIPTS

To make a game or tell a story, drag the blocks into a list with your mouse. The blocks clip together on the screen, a bit like real plastic blocks.

Lists are called *scripts*. When you click on a script, Scratch goes through the blocks one by one. The blocks move, change, spin, or check what a sprite is doing in the order you set.

Special blocks can repeat some or all of a script over and over or a set number of times. You can also make your script remember numbers and sentences and do simple math.

Moving one sprite around would make for boring stories, so you can have more than one sprite on the stage at a time. You can also set the stage background to make your story or game look more exciting.

FINDING AND STARTING SCRATCH

If your Pi isn't running, power it up and wait for the desktop to appear. Click the Menu button at the top left. Move the mouse down to Programming.

When the next menu slides out, move the mouse to Scratch. Click the Scratch item. After a while, the Scratch window appears.

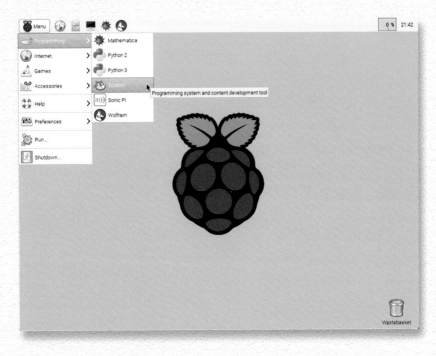

NOOBS sometimes moves things around. If you have a very new version, you may not see the same options on your Pi, or they may be in different places. Look for the words Programming and Scratch in the menu system to find them.

LOOKING AROUND SCRATCH

The Scratch window looks like it has a lot going on. But it doesn't really.

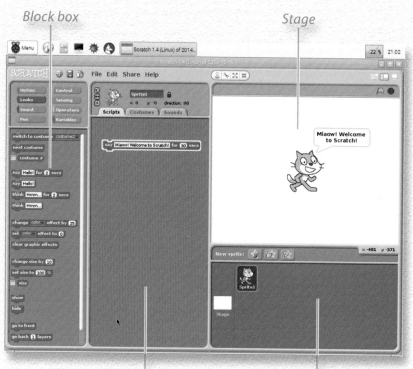

Block box

Stage

Script/Costume/Sounds box

Sprite Box

From left to right, look for four boxes:

» The block box has a list of all the blocks you can use. Blocks come in different colors, and the box shows only one color at a time.

» The Scripts/Costumes/Sounds box is where you clip blocks together to make scripts. You can also make new costumes — sprite shapes — and work with sounds by clicking the tags near the top of the box.

» The big white area with the cat is the Stage box. The stage is where you play your game or tell your story.

» The Sprite box is the area under the stage. It shows all the sprites in your story or game.

When you start Scratch, it makes a sprite for you. The sprite looks like a cartoon cat. You can change the way the sprite looks by changing its costume. You can make it move by changing its position on the stage.

UNDERSTANDING THE STAGE

The stage doesn't understand up, down, left, or right.

Instead, it uses a system with two magic numbers, so you can just tell a sprite to move to the right by some distance.

The numbers have special names: x and y.

The x number sets the left/right position. The y number sets the up/down position.

When x and y are both 0, the sprite is dead center of the stage. To move a sprite right, set x to more than 0.

What about left? You have to make the number less than 0 by putting a minus sign in front of it.

So when x is 100, the sprite is in the right half of the stage. When x is -100, it's in the left half of the stage.

Up and down work the same way. When y is 100, the sprite is in the top half. When y is -100, it's in the bottom half.

x and y are completely separate. They're independent, so you can move the sprite left or right without changing how far up or down it is. And you can move the sprite up and down without changing its left/right position. To move it up and down and left and right, you have to change x and y.

The following table has a cheat sheet.

MOVING ON THE STAGE WITH X AND Y

How Big Are x and y?	Where Is the Sprite?
x doesn't have a minus sign: 100	Right half of the stage
x has a minus sign: -100	Left half of the stage
y doesn't have a minus sign: 75	Top half of the stage
x has a minus sign: -75	Bottom half of the stage
x is zero: 0	Dead center left/right only
y is zero: 0	Dead center up/down only
x and y are zero: 0	Dead center left/right and up/down

Why does Scratch work like this? Wouldn't it be easier to say left, right, up, and down? It would. But x and y are borrowed from math. Grown-up game and app programming work the same way. Scratch copies how they work.

MOVING A SPRITE WITH GO TO

Let's try this out. If you can't see the blue blocks in the block list, click the blue Motion button near the top left of the stage.

Look down the list to find the block called go to. When you click it or include it in a script, it sets the x and y numbers that move a sprite.

You can see the x and y numbers in the block. Let's change them.

Double-click the x number. When it turns gray, type **200** and press Enter.

With a new x number, the sprite jumps toward the right of the screen. Cool! See how it works?

Now double-click the y number. When it turns gray, type -**100**.

The sprite moves down.

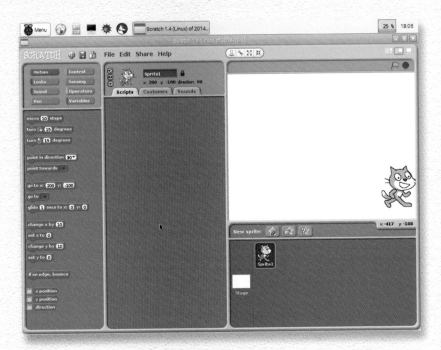

Your sprite may not be in the same place. The width and height of the stage depend on the width and height of your screen (monitor), so your stage may not be the same width and height as the stage in the image. You don't need to worry about where the sprite is, as long as it moves!

CENTERING A SPRITE

Can you work out how to use a go to block to move a sprite to the middle of the stage? There's a clue in the cheat sheet table in the earlier section, "Understanding the Stage."

You can probably guess that if you change x and y to 0, the sprite will jump back to the middle.

Now you can play with typing other numbers into the x and y boxes to see what they do. After a while, you should be able to guess what a number does before you try it.

If you look at the block list, you can see other blocks you can use now. Click once on the following to see what they do:

```
change x by [number]
set x to [number]
change y by [number]
set y to [number]
```

GLIDING A SPRITE

People and things in the real world don't usually jump instantly from one place to another. (It would be good if they did. But they don't.)

To make movement look more realistic, you can use the `glide` block. It works like the `go to` block, but it has an extra number in seconds. The extra number sets how long it takes the sprite to move.

Try changing the x and y numbers and the time in seconds in the `glide` block to see what it does.

MOVING AND TURNING A SPRITE

Scratch gives you another way to move sprites. Instead of moving to somewhere on the stage, you can tell a sprite to move in the direction it's facing. You can also turn it to make it face in a different direction.

Use the `move`, `turn`, and `point` blocks to move like this. They're at the top of the block list. Try clicking on them and changing the numbers in them to see what they do.

There's also a `point in direction` block that makes the sprite turn to face the direction you set. The direction is set in degrees, which are like small turning steps. Type **360** degrees to turn the sprite all the way around.

You can click the number box to set your own number, or you can select four directions from a menu. See whether you can work out which numbers mean left, right, up, and down.

UNDERSTANDING TURN AND ROTATION

If you turn a sprite, it may not turn on the stage, even though it's pointing in a new direction. This may be confusing, because although the sprite has turned because you told it to, it still looks like it's facing the same way!

The complicated math-y word for turning something is *rotation*. Scratch gives you a choice about how the sprite looks when you rotate it.

If you look closely, you can see three tiny buttons to the left of the sprite in the top part of the middle window.

You can click any button to select it.

From top to bottom, they work like this:

» **can rotate.** Click this button to make sure the sprite always turns. It can face up, down, left, right, or any direction in between. Sometimes this means it's upside down.

» **only face left/right.** The sprite only faces left or right, even if it's pointing up or down. It's never upside down.

» **don't rotate.** The sprite always faces the same way. You can still change its direction. But you only ever see one direction on the stage.

MAKING A SIMPLE SCRIPT

You can make a simple script by dragging blocks to the Scripts area in the middle of the screen.

Try this:

1 Drag a move **block to the script area.**

2 Drag a turn **block to the script area and hold it just under the** move **block without lifting your finger from the mouse button.**

As you drag a block, Scratch highlights it by drawing a white line around it.

When you let go of the mouse button, the bottom block clips to the top block.

You made a script! When you click anywhere on the script, Scratch steps through each block in turn. This script makes the sprite move, and then it makes it turn.

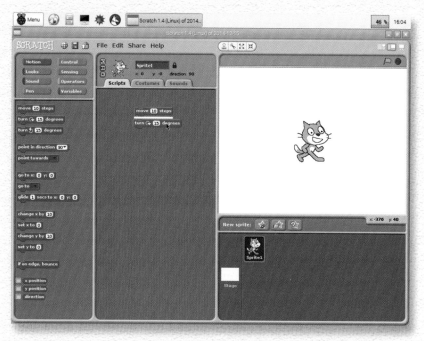

This is a very simple script with only a couple of blocks, but Scratch works the same way with longer scripts: It starts at the top, does what each block tells it to, then moves to the next block, does what that block says, and so on, all the way down the list of blocks.

Making a script work is called *running a script*. Imagine a script wizard running from the top of the script to the bottom and making each block work in turn. Scripts work like that, only the wizard is invisible and isn't really a wizard. (Well, maybe a bit.)

You can clip blocks to the top of a script as well as the bottom. You can clip a block whenever it has a slot or a tag.

BREAKING UP A SCRIPT

Sometimes you want to split up a script. Maybe you want to take off the last few blocks. Or maybe you want to make a gap in the middle so that you can put more blocks in.

To break a script, click on a block and drag it. The script splits, and Scratch shows the white line. Drag the block far enough — it doesn't matter where, as long as it's away from the script — and the white box vanishes. Now you have two blocks, or maybe two smaller scripts.

RIGHT-CLICKING ON BLOCKS

Scratch has some cool extra tools. To see them, right-click on a block or a script.

» Click Help to get a hint about what a block does. The hint appears in a window. Click OK to make the window go away.

» Click Duplicate to make a copy of a script or block. The copy appears in the script area.

» Click Delete to get rid of a script or block from the script area. The block or script disappears. If you do this by accident and change your mind, choose Edit ⇨ Undelete from the menu at the top of the Scratch window to make the script/block reappear.

MAKING A RESET SCRIPT FOR A SPRITE

Can you work out how to make a reset script to move it back to its starting point and make it face the right way now? You want to join two blocks to move the sprite to x:0 and y:0 and turn it so that it faces to the right.

Try clipping blocks together and changing the numbers inside them until you've made a script that does this. Remember, you can have more than one script in the script area at a time, so you can make this script and reuse it later. It will be useful!

CONTROLLING A SCRIPT

Sometimes you want a script to do something over and over. If you broke up the script in the previous section, put it back together.

Click on it a few times. The sprite moves and turns each time. So . . . you can make a script do the same thing over and over by clicking it over and over.

That works fine for a few repeats. But what if you want to repeat something hundreds of times?

You could use the Duplicate right-click tool to make lots and lots of copies of your simple script and clip them together to make one big script.

That works for maybe ten repeats. But it's a boring way to make a script do something hundreds of times.

Scratch has a better way. Click the Control button at the top of the block library. (It has an orange edge.) When you click it, you see a new set of blocks.

These are control blocks. They make your scripts smarter. You can use control blocks do things like

» Repeat some blocks forever.

» Repeat some blocks a set number of times and then carry on.

» Start a script when you press a key.

» Make a script wait for a set time, like a second or a minute.

» Make a script wait until something else happens, like maybe two sprites colliding.

» Repeat a script until something else happens.

» Check and test numbers, sprite positions, and other things.

» Stop a script.

» Stop all scripts.

USING CONTROL BLOCKS

Control blocks go in three places:

» At the start of a script

» At the end of a script

» Around other blocks

Start control blocks have a round top. You can't clip a block on top of them. They have to go first because they wait for something to happen. The script can't start until it happens!

For example, the when [space] key pressed block starts a script when you press the space key. You can pick a different key using the menu in the block.

End control blocks have a flat bottom. You can't clip a block under them. They have to go at the end of a script because they tell the script to stop.

Around blocks have a space inside them. They look a bit like fat hairclips. To use them, drag them around the script you want to control.

You may have to split the script to pull out the blocks you want to control first and then glue it back together after you added the around control block.

Let's try out the repeat block. Drag it from the block list to the script area and clip it around the two blocks there already. The bottom end of the clip stretches to fit around the blocks.

Click the block, and the sprite moves and turns.

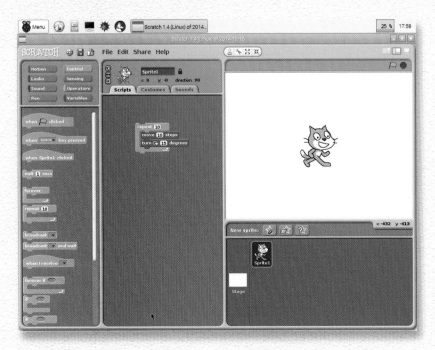

 If your sprite doesn't turn, check which rotation button is lit. For details, see the earlier "Understanding turn and rotation" section.

STOPPING SCRIPTS

Click the number in the `repeat` block, type **100**, and press Enter. Click the script again.

Now the sprite moves and turns over and over. It keeps moving for a long time.

Did you get bored? If you want to stop a script early, you can click the red button above the stage. The green flag next to it lights up when a script is running.

You can also click a script to stop it. While it's running, you can see a white border around it. When you stop it, the border disappears.

MAKING A SIMPLE BOUNCE SCRIPT

Can you make a script that bounces the sprite off the edges of the screen? There's an easy way, and a hard way, to do this.

The easy way is to use the if on edge, bounce block in the Motion block list. Clip a move block and the if on edge, bounce block together. Put them inside a forever control block.

If you worked out how to make a reset script, click it to move the sprite to the middle of the screen. (If not, see the earlier "Making a reset script for a sprite" section.)

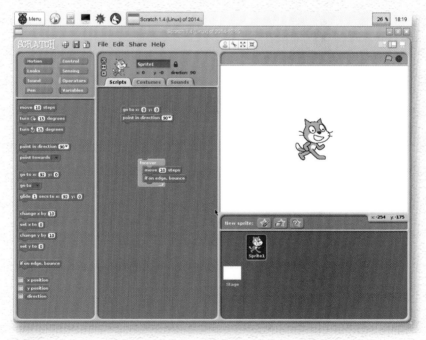

 You can click the middle only face left-right rotation button to keep the sprite the right way up when it bounces.

Click the script. The sprite should bounce between the two sides of the stage! Click the script again to stop it.

What happens if you turn the sprite first? Click a turn block to turn the sprite.

To allow the sprite to turn, you must have the Can Rotate button selected. Remember, it's the top one of the group of three to the left of the sprite at the top of the script area.

Click the script to run it again. The sprite bounces up and down and left and right! Click the script to stop it.

INTRODUCING VARIABLES

What does bounce do? What happens when the sprite bounces?

If you think about it, a *bounce* means your sprite turns to face the other way, so you could use a turn block to make it bounce. You could tell the sprite to face left when it bounces off the right edge of the screen and to face right when it bounces off the left edge.

But maybe you want to make the sprite do something else — like jump when you press one key, hide behind another sprite when you press a different key, or bounce before it hits the edge.

To do that, you need to know where your sprite is, and you have to be able to change where it is.

You could make a lot of `go to` blocks with a different x and y for every place on the stage the sprite might be. But that would be a *lot* of blocks.

A better way would be to change x and y positions as needed. You can do this in Scratch using variable blocks.

A *variable* is like a box that holds a number. The box has a name, so you can tell it from other boxes. And it has space for a number.

Variables can remember letters, words, and sentences, too — but don't worry about this yet.

USING VARIABLES

Variables have special blocks, and when you make one variable, you get some extra special blocks to help you use it. You can set the variable to a number or add a number to it.

When you make a variable, it appears on the stage. You don't always want this, so you can use a `hide variable` block to make it go away. You can use a `show variable` block to make it come back.

Variables can do math! You can add, subtract, multiply, and divide variables. You can even add, subtract, multiply, and divide one variable by another!

Best of all, you can use a variable wherever you see a number. For example, you can tell a `go to` block to use a variable you make. When you click the `go to` block or when Scratch reaches it in a script, the block moves the sprite to the number stored in the variable.

Variables give you way more options than moving a sprite to the same place all the time.

MAKING A VARIABLE

To make a variable, click the darker orange Variables button at the bottom right of the block types in the block list area. Two buttons appear. You can click them to

» Make a variable

» Make a list

After you make a variable, another button, called Delete a variable, appears in the list. You can click it to get rid of a variable you're not using anymore.

Click the `Make a variable` block. Type **sprite1_x** into the Variable name? box. Leave the For all sprites option checked. Click OK.

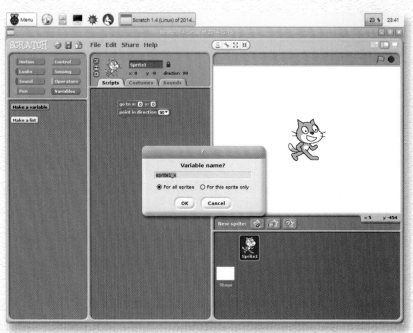

Whoa! Stuff happens! Scratch makes some new blocks. And if you look at the stage, you'll see a box appears, with the name of your variable — `sprite1_x` — and a number.

When you make a new variable, the number is always 0 because you haven't changed it yet.

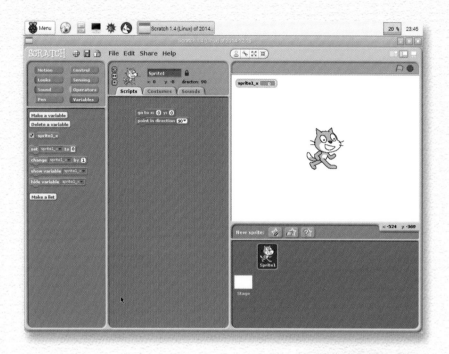

LISTS

A list is a special kind of a variable that holds other variables. It's like a big box with lots of smaller boxes inside it.

They're numbered so that you can tell them apart and do clever things like add a number to the third box in the list. Lists are a bit cleverer than plain variables. You don't need lists yet, but feel free to play with them if you like.

Can you use variables to replace any number? You totally can! You can use a `set` block to set a variable to the value of another variable. In a `change` block, you can make the `by` value a variable. You can make scripts that are really smart, with variables passing values to other variables between sprites all over the stage. There are almost no limits to what you can do.

UNDERSTANDING FOR ALL SPRITES AND THIS SPRITE ONLY

When you make a variable, you can tell Scratch to make it *private* for each sprite by clicking the For this sprite only option. If it's private, other sprites can't read it, change, or even see it.

Sometimes private is a good thing. It means you can use the same variable names in different sprites, so you can copy a script and use it with a new sprite without changing anything.

But sometimes you want one sprite to know what's happening in the scripts for another sprite. That's when you leave For all sprites selected as you make the variable. Now you can use the variable in every script for every sprite.

This looks like something you can ignore, but it's a big deal. Programmers spend a lot of time thinking about whether to make variables private or public. If you make everything public, you can make a big mess and never be sure which script is changing which variable. If you have too many private variables, you can't get at the variables you need. You don't need to worry about this for simple scripts, but it's something to remember when your scripts get very big.

PLUGGING VARIABLES INTO BLOCKS

The big deal about variables is that you can use them to replace numbers. Instead of a fixed number like 10, which never changes, you can use a variable that you control with the power of control blocks and math.

Scratch does some clever tricks to make this work. You can literally drag and drop a variable on top of a number to replace it. Let's try it.

Drag your `sprite1_x` variable block and drop it into the script window.

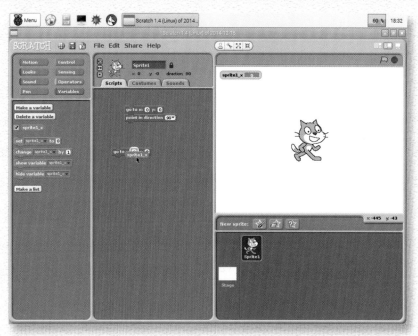

Ignore the set, change, show, and hide blocks. You want the block with the variable name and nothing else.

Now click the Motion block type at the top left of the block list window, and drag a `go to` block onto the script window.

And for your next trick, drag the `variable` block and drop it on the white number box. If you do it right, the variable replaces the 0 that used to be there.

SETTING AND CHANGING THE VARIABLE VALUE

The number inside the variable is called the *value*. Click the Variables button at the top of the block list and find the set and change blocks.

When you click a set block or use it in a script, it sets the value to the number in the block.

When you click a change block or use it in a script, it adds the number after by to the value. When you start, that number is 1, so the block adds 1 to a value. But you can click it and change it.

Try it now. Click the number in the set block and change it to, say, 10. Click the set block and watch what happens.

Click the change block a few times. Did you see what happened? The sprite1_x value box on the stage changed when you clicked the blocks.

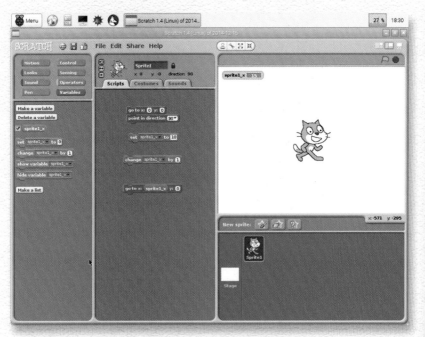

The set and change blocks are in the script area so that you can see them more clearly. You don't need to copy them to use them. You can click them and change the numbers inside them in the block list. But often, if you're playing with blocks, it's good to make a copy in the script area so that you can change them and maybe plug them into a script when you're done.

UNDERSTANDING VARIABLES IN BLOCKS

Something didn't happen — the sprite didn't move. Why not?

The `go to` block moves the sprite only when you click on it or when Scratch runs it as part of a script. It doesn't move the sprite when you change a variable inside it.

You might think it would, but it doesn't — for a good reason.

You want to be able to change a value without lots of stuff happening as a result. Scratch works better if it does only the stuff you tell it to, not stuff you might want, maybe.

So if you want a sprite to move, you have to set a variable in the `go to` block and then click the block or run it inside a script. Otherwise, no movement.

Other blocks work the same way. They read the variable value only when they're in a script and it runs, or you click them.

SHOWING AND HIDING VARIABLES

What do you think happens if you click on the `show variable` and `hide variable` blocks? Try it now!

Was that a surprise? `hide variable` hides the value box on the stage. `show variable` makes it appear on the stage.

You can use these blocks to clean up the stage when you have so many variables it looks like a mess. You don't usually need to look at all the values at once. Sometimes you don't need to look at the values at all — which is when you need these blocks.

PROJECT 4 MEET SONIC PI

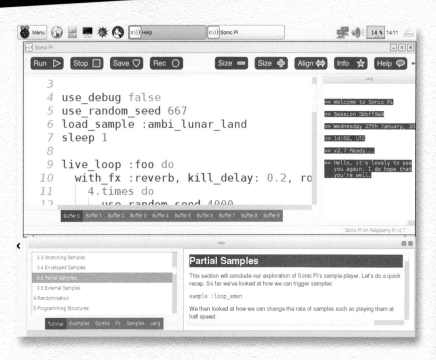

SONIC PI IS A FREE MUSIC SYNTHESIZER AND SEQUENCER. You don't play it from a keyboard or other instrument. You play it by writing code.

If you're not into music, Sonic Pi is a cool way to make some weird sounds. And if you are into music, the only limit is your imagination!

Sonic Pi code is a bit more complicated than Scratch (see Project 3) because instead of clicking blocks together, you have to type the magic words.

But the idea is the same. When you tell Sonic Pi to run some code, it goes through it line by line and does whatever the code tells it to do.

There's a lot to learn in Sonic Pi, but you don't have to learn all of it at once! This project is just a taster to get you started. If you want to master Sonic Pi, you can work through the tutorials (lessons) built into it.

GETTING STARTED WITH SONIC PI

To launch Sonic Pi, click the Menu button at the top left and choose Programming ➪ Sonic Pi.

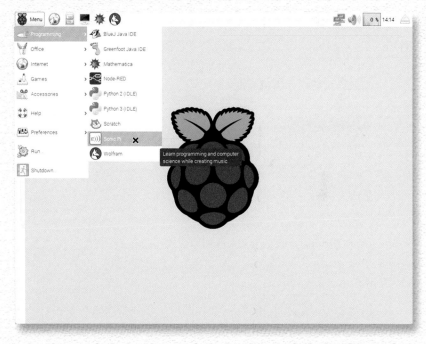

Sonic Pi takes a while to load. When the splash screen with the logo and the information about Sonic Pi disappears, click the second button at the top right of the window bar.

The size of the window changes. You should see a line of buttons labeled Buffer 0 to Buffer 9 under the main window at the top left.

If you can't see the buttons, grab the top of the Help window and drag it down until they appear. Then click the bottom right of the main window to make it smaller.

When you're done, drag the Help window back up.

SETTING UP SOUND ON THE PI

Sound on the Pi just works — mostly. You may need to experiment with the Sonic Pi settings — called Prefs or Preferences — depending on the hardware you use to listen to the sound.

To show the Prefs, click the tiny arrows at the far right of the bar with the buttons at the top of the window. The arrows are next to the Help button.

When a button labeled Prefs appears, click it. You can use the Raspberry Pi System Volume Slider to set the volume.

The sound quality of the Pi's headphone socket isn't brilliant. And because the Pi is a slow computer, you can't make really big, fat, complicated sounds with it. But you can still have a lot of fun playing with note patterns, synths, samples, and FX — even if you don't know much about music or have never tried to play an instrument.

If you don't hear any sound when you use Sonic Pi, you probably need to select a different item in the Raspberry Pi Audio Output box.

If you have a TV or monitor connected but you want to listen through the Pi's headphone socket, click the Headphones item.

If you want to listen to the sound through your TV or monitor speakers, click the HDMI button. If you leave the setting unchanged, the Pi guesses what you want.

If you have a screen connected with an HDMI lead and it doesn't have speakers, you may not hear anything unless you change the Prefs to send the sound to the headphones.

Click the tiny cross at the top right of the Prefs when you have finished.

The easy way to hear sound is to plug some headphones or earbuds into the socket on the side of the Pi. If you have some speakers, you can plug them in to the same socket. Keep the volume down at first! Turn it up to a comfortable level using the Prefs so that you don't deafen yourself.

PLAYING TUNES WITH SONIC PI

Before the guided tour, let's make some simple music.

1 Launch Sonic Pi, if you haven't already.

When you launch Sonic Pi, you should see Welcome to Sonic Pi in the main editor window.

2 Type this code on the next line:

```
play 70
```

See that line that starts with a hash (#)? That's called a comment. *Comments are for display only, for you. They don't do anything else. Add them to your code to remind yourself what it does. A year from now when you look at your code, you won't be able to remember how it works. That's why you need comments.*

3 Click the Run button at the top left.

Did you hear a note? If you didn't hear anything, go back to the Prefs and experiment with the settings until clicking Run makes a noise.

4 If you heard a note, click in the Programming Panel and press the Backspace key a couple of times to delete 70.

5 Now type 60 instead so that the code looks like this:

```
play 60
```

6 Click Run again.

Can you hear how the note changed? The sound — the *pitch* — is lower.

PLAYING NOTES TOGETHER

You can play notes together.

1 Edit the code so that it looks like the following and click Run:

```
play 60
```

```
play 64
play 67
```

Those notes make a nice sound.

2 **Edit the code so it looks like this and click Run again:**

```
play 60
play 61
play 62
play 63
play 64
play 65
```

That's not such a nice sound, is it?

Musicians know which notes sound good together and which notes don't. Music that sounds nice all the time is boring, so most music has a mix of nice and not-so-nice note combinations.

PLAYING WITH TIME

You don't have to play all the notes at the same time. You can tell Sonic Pi to take a nap between notes, like this:

```
play 60
sleep 1
play 64
sleep 1
play 67
```

Sonic Pi reads the 1 as 1 whole beat. Most music uses shorter notes. You usually divide beats into half-beats, quarter-beats, and eighth-beats. For very fast music, you can use sixteenths, or even 30 seconds.

How long is a beat? A lot of dance music has a thump-thump-thump-thump bass drum. That's what four beats sound like.

Because Sonic Pi was made by programmers and not musicians, you have to give it a beat fraction as a decimal number. This table is a cheat sheet for beat counting.

NEAT BEAT CHEAT SHEET

Beat Fraction	Sleep Time
1	1
Half	0.5
Quarter	0.25
Eighth	0.125
Sixteenth	0.0625
Thirty-second	0.03125

Try the following:

```
play 60
sleep 0.125
play 64
sleep 0.5
play 67
sleep 0.25
play 64
sleep 0.125
play 60
```

Using different beats creates a rhythm, which makes a tune more interesting.

Beats work well when all the numbers add up to a whole number — 1, 2, and so on. They don't have to, but strange things happen if you try to play tunes with a different number of beats at the same time.

TAKING A GUIDED TOUR

After you've made some noise, let's look at the features you can see in the Sonic Pi window.

You can move and resize some of Sonic Pi's windows. Click and drag one of the dividers between areas to resize. If you get it right, the cursor changes to show you that you can move the divider.

LOOKING AT THE PROGRAMMING PANEL

The area where you type code is officially called the Programming Panel. Because you can edit — change — the code, it's also called the Editor window, or sometimes just the Code window.

Sonic Pi is designed for live coding, which means you can try out sounds and note patterns without stopping other sounds and note patterns.

Simple? It is. But notice the buttons under the window labeled with Buffer and a number. *Buffer* is really just a special way to say project.

You can use the eight buffers to edit up to eight projects at the same time.

Click any of the buffer buttons. The Programming Panel shows the code for that project.

Does that mean you can play eight projects at the same time? Yes, it does! That's why live coding is so cool — you can make an entire band out of software and make each part start, stop, or play something different.

And Sonic Pi remembers the buffers when you quit. The next time you play with Sonic Pi, your code is still there!

If you make a mistake in your code, Sonic Pi makes a special window appear under the Programming Panel, with some cryptic messages to tell you more about why your code doesn't work. The messages aren't easy to understand, but sometimes they give you enough of a clue to fix the problem.

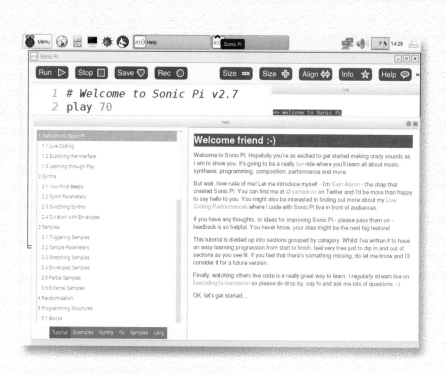

LOOKING AT THE LOG WINDOW

The Log Window shows messages from Sonic Pi. When Sonic Pi plays a note, it adds a message to the window. When you know more about Sonic Pi, you can write your own messages to the window as reminders to yourself. Mostly you can ignore what happens in this window.

UNDERSTANDING THE HELP WINDOW

At the bottom of the screen is a Help Window with more buttons along the bottom. It has two sections.

The small window at the left is a list of all the features in Sonic Pi, collected into groups.

When you click a button at the bottom of the left window, the bigger window at the right shows more information about it.

Here's a list of buttons:

» **Tutorial:** Step-by-step lessons you can try

» **Examples:** Ready-made projects

» **Synths:** Ready-made electronic sounds to make bass notes, bells, whooshes, beeps, growls, and other noises

» **FX:** Ready-made electronic sound changers that process the sound and make it more interesting (or turn it into a grungey distorted mess — but sometimes you want that, so it's cool)

» **Samples:** A different collection of ready-made sounds (unlike synths, which make sounds by doing lots of scary math, samples are recordings of drum sounds, looped rhythms, ambient sounds for atmosphere, and the like)

» **Lang:** Short for Language — this button lists all the commands and special words you can use in Sonic Pi code

On a small screen, you can see only some of the buttons. If you move the mouse to the top of the Help bar, the cursor changes into a double arrow. Now you can drag the top of the Help window up and down to show more of the Help buttons and less of the Programming Panel.

You can listen to the Tutorial and Example code. Click-drag the mouse to highlight the code — it's red in the tutorials, blue in the examples. Right-click and choose Copy. Select a blank workspace, right-click, and choose Paste. Then click Run. To clear a workspace, right-click, choose Clear All, and press Delete.

UNDERSTANDING THE TOOLS

There's yet another row of much bigger buttons along the top of the window. These are the Sonic Pi Tools. They control the main features of Sonic Pi.

Most Tools do more or less what you expect. A few have some not-so-obvious gotcha features.

» **Run:** Play the code in the current project.

» **Stop:** Stop the code in the current project.

» **Save:** Save the code in the current project.

» **Rec:** Record the sound. When you click Stop, Sonic Pi asks for a filename so that you can save the file.

» **Size +** and **Size -:** Make the code in the Programming Panel bigger or smaller. This doesn't change the sound; it just makes it easier or harder to see and edit the code.

» **Align:** Apply some magic to make code in the workspace line up the way it should.

» **Info:** Shows an info window about Sonic Pi. You won't need to click this button more than once.

» **Help:** Shows/hides the Help area.

» **Prefs:** Sets up sound on the Pi. If you use the Pi with a small screen, you can see this button only if you click the double arrows at the far right of the Tools area.

If you're not careful, you can make the Tools disappear. To make them reappear, click on the bar to the right of Log in the Log window and click Tools in the menu that appears.

As of version 2.9 of Sonic Pi, you can't load the code you save. This may be fixed in a future version.

UNDERSTANDING CODE COMPLETION

When you type a command into the Programming Panel, Sonic Pi tries to guess the rest of it. It doesn't make very smart guesses — it shows possible code alphabetically in a floating menu next to the code.

You can either scroll through the menu with the mouse to pick a command, or you can keep typing to narrow down the options. When the menu highlights the command you want, press Enter, and Sonic Pi types the rest of it for you.

This feature is called *code completion*. Many of the code editors used by professional developers include it. It can be a real timesaver, so it's a good idea to get used to working with code completion.

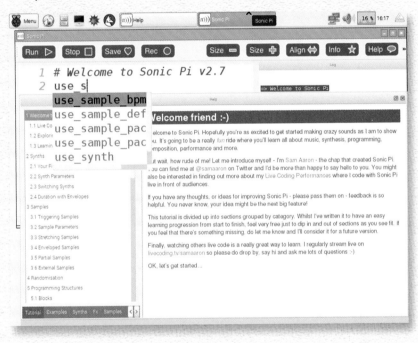

UNDERSTANDING NOTES

You don't need to know a lot about music to make sounds with Sonic Pi. But it helps to know what the different features do.

USING NOTE NUMBERS

Music is made of notes. There's more than one way to tell Sonic Pi which notes to play.

Note numbers have a range of 0 to 127. You don't usually use note numbers lower than 24, because they sound muddy — or so low you can't hear them! Note numbers over 100 are so high they can hurt your ears.

Tunes often sound good with numbers between 40 and 70, but this is just a rough guide, not a rule.

Note numbers don't have to be whole numbers. You can do this:

```
play 59.95
play 60
play 60.05
```

Playing groups of note numbers with small differences is a good way to make big, thick, interesting sounds.

USING NOTE NAMES

If you know something about music, you can use the usual note letter names ABCDEFG with a colon (:) in front, like this:

```
play :e
```

You can add a number between 0 and 10, called an *octave,* which makes the pitch lower or higher.

```
play :e2
play :e5
```

Octaves have a weird magic property. In a mysterious way, notes with the same letter are the same note, even though they have a different pitch.

You can also add a sharp (s) to make the pitch a little higher or a flat (b) to make the pitch a little lower:

```
play :c
play :cs
play :cb
```

MAKING DIFFERENT SOUNDS

To make music in Sonic Pi, you use code to pick and play notes, and then you send the notes to synths or samples to make a sound.

To use a synth, the command is

```
use_synth :synth_name
```

Click the Synths tab in the left Help window to see a list of names.

The colon (:) goes before the synth name, with no space. It doesn't go on the end of use_synth. *You'll probably get this wrong a few times before you remember it.*

You can make little tunes by playing the same note with different synths:

```
use_synth :fm
play 60
sleep 0.25
use_synth :mod_beep
play 60
sleep 0.25
use_synth :growl
play 60
sleep 0.25
use_synth :hollow
play 60
```

USING SYNTH PARAMETERS

Synths have settings that change the sound. The settings are called *parameters,* which is a math-y word used in Music Land to mean setting.

Some settings, like volume and left/right speaker position, are used in almost all synths.

Sometimes the names are different. Volume can be called level *or* amplitude. *In Sonic Pi, it's called* amp. *Left/right position is usually called* panning *or* pan, *which sounds like the Sonic Pi has escaped from your kitchen, but has nothing to do with cooking.*

Other settings are unique to each synth. You can see the list of settings for each synth on the Help pages.

To play with parameters, add them to a note, like this:

```
play 60, amp: 0.1
```

If you want to use more parameters, separate them with commas:

```
play 60, amp: 0.1, pan: -1
```

The table has a list of parameters that work on most synths. attack, decay, and release take a time in seconds, from 0 to however long you want to wait.

SORT OF STANDARD SYNTH PARAMETERS

Parameter Name	What Does It Do, and What's the Range?
amp	Sets the volume: 0 to 1.
pan	Moves the sound between the speakers: -1 to 1.
attack	Controls how quickly the sound starts.
decay	Controls how quickly the sound reaches the sustain volume after it starts.
sustain	Volume after the decay time: 0 to 1. This volume stays the same as long as the note lasts.
release	Controls how quickly the sound dies away.

You can make sounds that take minutes to get started and hours to die away. They're not very fun to listen to, but if you want to do it, Sonic Pi makes it possible.

UNDERSTANDING DEFAULT PARAMETERS

Synths have parameter settings baked in. When you play a synth, it uses these default numbers for its settings, unless you add your own settings to a note.

To see a list of parameters and default settings, click the Synth tab in the left Help window and click any synth from the list. The boxes under the name show all the parameter names you can use for that synth and the default settings for each parameter.

For example, if you look up the synth called `dsaw`, you can see that the default `sustain` value is 0, the default `cutoff` is 100, and so on.

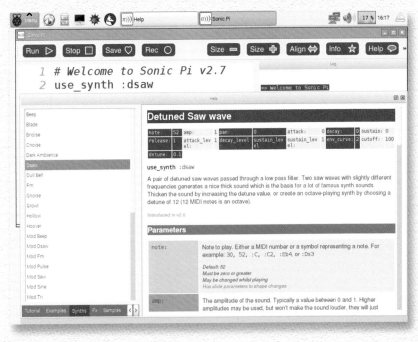

If you don't know what a parameter does, try playing it with different settings to see how the sound changes.

Synth parameter names are based on those used in hardware synthesizers and in electronic music plug-ins, so if you want to know more, you can try searching for the parameter name online.

MAKING MORE COMPLICATED MUSIC

If you read the earlier sections in this project, you know enough now to start making simple tracks. You can create some very cool effects just by switching synths and changing parameters, even if you play the same note over and over.

If you know a bit about music, you can pick note numbers and letter names to make tunes and play lots of notes together to make chords.

If you don't, you can mess around randomly. With a bit of fooling around, you can usually make something good.

REPEATING NOTES AND SECTIONS

A lot of music has repeats. Of course, you can repeat sections by copying and pasting them. But that's a slow way to work, and if you want to make a change in one section, you have to copy it to every other section.

Repeats are easy in Sonic Pi. You just do them, like this:

```
2.times do
  play 60
  sleep 0.25
  play 67
  sleep 0.25
end
```

Sonic Pi repeats the section between do and end twice. If you want more repeats, change the 2 at the start to some other number.

If you want the loop to repeat forever — or at least until someone comes into your room and unplugs your Pi to turn the noise off, or you get bored and click Stop — replace the 2.times command with a loop command.

```
loop do  # Repeat forever...
  play 60
  sleep 2
end
```

You can type spaces on each line of the do block by hand, but it's much easier to type the code without spaces and then click the Align button in the tools. Magic! You get neat spaces without extra typing.

NESTING REPEATS

You can put repeats inside repeats. This is called *nesting* because "putting repeats inside other repeats and so on" has way too many words, and it's no fun typing it over and over. The figure has an example.

```
1 # Welcome to Sonic Pi v2.7
2 4.times do
3   play 60
4   sleep 0.25
5   2.times do
6     play 64
7     sleep 0.25
8   end
9   2.times do
10    play 67
11    sleep 0.25
12  end
13 end
```

```
4.times do
  play 60
  sleep 0.25
  2.times do
    play 64
    sleep 0.25
  end
  2.times do
    play 67
    sleep 0.25
  end
end
```

To get nesting to work, you have to match every do with an end. This is where the Align button is really handy. Again.

To make sections of music, you put more complicated code between the repeats. Sonic Pi doesn't care how long each block is. When you make a list of nested blocks, Sonic Pi always runs through them in order.

You can see the notes appear in the Log window as they play.

SAVING AND LOADING

You can save code by clicking the Save button and saving it to a file. It's a good idea to save files with a .sonic extension so that you know what they are. If you know how to make a folder for files, make one and save them there. Otherwise, they can go on the desktop.

How do you load a file? You can't!

(Continued)

(Continued)

Lots of things about Sonic Pi are very clever. This isn't one of them. It's really dumb. But there is a work-around.

To load a file, do the following:

1 At the top of the screen, outside the Sonic Pi window, click the Menu button. Then choose Accessories ⇨ Text Editor.

2 In the text editor, choose File ⇨ Open.

3 Find a file you saved.

4 Click it with the mouse and click Open at the bottom right.

5 When the editor loads your code, drag the mouse over it to select it all.

6 Right-click and choose Copy.

7 Click the cross near the top right to close the Editor window.

8 Click back to Sonic Pi.

9 Click a buffer to select it.

10 Right-click and choose Select All.

11 Right-click and choose Paste.

The code you saved should appear in the buffer, and you can carry on coding.

The Help files mention you can share code using a website called GitHub (https://github.com). You can. You can also save and load files. But GitHub is really complicated. If you want a challenge, you can research how to use it. But don't worry if you get stuck. It's not easy!

PROJECT 5 PICK UP PYTHON

```
for letter in 'Python':
        print 'Current letter is: ', letter
```

```
Python 2.7.9 (default, Mar  8 2015, 00:52:26)
[GCC 4.9.2] on linux2
Type "copyright", "credits" or "license()" for more information.
>>> =============================== RESTART ===============================
===
>>>
Current letter is:  P
Current letter is:  y
Current letter is:  t
Current letter is:  h
Current letter is:  o
Current letter is:  n
>>> |
```

YOU CAN MAYBE GUESS FROM SCRATCH AND SONIC PI THAT THERE ARE LOTS OF WAYS TO MAKE A COMPUTER DO WHAT YOU WANT. Technically, Scratch and Sonic Pi are called computer languages. Experts love creating new languages, so there are literally hundreds of different ones.

This project introduces a popular language called Python. Unlike some languages, Python is easy to learn. But it's a real grown-up language used by real grown-up programmers. Python is a big language with lots of features, and this project gives you a quick taste of Python programming — enough to get you started. If you want to know more, you can search online for Python (and ignore the photos of snakes).

MEET PYTHON

Scratch is a good way to start learning about programming, but there's a lot you can't do with Scratch. For example, you can't create your own desktop windows, search web pages for information, or send tweets.

For bigger and smarter projects, you need a bigger and smarter way to give your computer instructions, which you can do in lots of ways. One of the most popular methods is to type your instructions using a programming language.

A *programming language* takes your instructions and tries to understand them. If your instructions make sense, the programming language tells the chips and other parts of the computer what they need to do.

Programming languages save you time because you don't have to think about all the complicated things the computer is doing while it works. You can use instructions that look a bit like English, and the programming language does the rest.

Although Scratch is a very simple programming language, it's very unusual. Most languages don't give you instruction blocks you can clip together. Instead, you write *commands* — special words that tell the computer what you want it to do. The list of commands you write is called *code.*

You can't make mistakes or typos in code, so copy everything in this project exactly. If the code uses small letters, use small letters. If it uses big letters, use big letters. When it has both, use both and don't change them. If it has punctuation marks, make sure you copy them. Don't leave anything out. Don't add anything. Don't change anything at all, or the code may not work.

To make a program, you type code on the keyboard into an *editor.* An editor is a bit like a notepad application or a word processor, but it has special features to help you write code.

Some editors can even run code for you so that you can check whether it works right away. Python's editor can do this. An editor that runs commands and code is sometimes called a *shell*.

You won't hear the sea if you hold the Pi up to your ear, but you can use the Python shell for quick math like a calculator and to run simple Python one-line commands.

In other languages, a shell is sometimes called a REPL, which is short for Read Eval Print Loop. It's also called an interpreter. The words all mean more or less the same thing. (Experts like to argue about the tiny differences, but you can ignore the differences. And the experts.)

FIND PYTHON ON THE PI

Python and a Python editor are built into your Pi, so you don't have to do anything complicated or clever to make them work. Just click the Menu button, hover over Programming, and choose Python 2 (IDLE) in the menu.

Don't click Python 3 (IDLE). It launches a different, less popular version of Python. If you try to use it, some of the code in this project won't work. This will make both of us unhappy, so don't click that icon!

IDLE doesn't mean Python is lazy. It's short for Integrated Development and Learning Environment, which is a long and complicated way of saying "An Editor for Python."

You maybe noticed that the date at the top of the window isn't the current date. It's the date when the people who made Python released it into the world for everyone to use. Some people get confused by this date, so it's good to unconfuse them.

After a few seconds of tense and anxious waiting during which your Pi appears to be doing nothing, a Python window appears!

You can see some technical looking words at the top. They more or less just mean "Okay, I'm Python, and I'm ready to do useful things."

When you see the >>> arrows, Python is ready, and you can start typing — unless you have a small monitor and the text is too small for you. If you do, let's fix that.

SET UP PYTHON

If you have a wall-sized super-monitor and can read the text just fine, skip to the next section. Otherwise, do the following:

1 In the menu at the top of the Python window, click Options.

2 Click Configure IDLE when it appears under Options.

A big box appears with settings and all kinds of other options.

3 Click the box labeled Size.

4 Select a number in the drop-down list.

Picking a bigger number makes the letters and words bigger in the Python window.

5 Click Ok to set the new size.

The *default* size — the one that's preselected for you — is 10. To make the text bigger, select a bigger number. The Python examples in this book use size 20, which is very, very big to make sure you can read them. Try size 12 or 14.

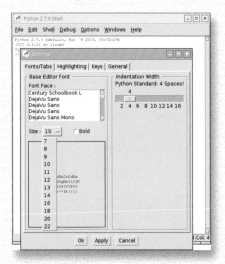

When you change the text size, the text gets bigger. And the window gets bigger, too. If you make the text really big, the window may not fit on the screen. This doesn't usually cause issues, but it can look kind of weird and disturbing. If the window is toooooo wiiiiide, you can't see all the text in it, which is not what you want. You can fix this by dragging the corners of the window to make it smaller.

UNLEASH PYTHON MATH POWER

Now you can unleash the full power of Python supercomputing. The line with the angle brackets is called a *prompt*. It's like the Linux command prompt, except that it sends commands to Python instead of Linux.

Type the following at the prompt and then press Enter:

```
>>>1+1
```

Woo hoo! Python instantly solves this tough problem. It even displays another prompt to prove it's totally not scared of math.

```
2
>>>
```

Obviously, Python can do harder math. Try something like

```
>>>1/81.0*100
```

Don't forget to press Enter. You'll see that Python has no problem with more complicated sums.

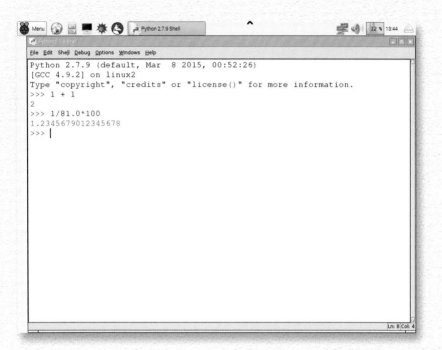

Python is more accurate than a basic calculator. Try the same sum on a calculator, and you get a shorter and less precise answer. This small difference doesn't matter for simple classroom math, but some college-level math problems need very accurate answers. A calculator isn't good enough — but Python is.

In Python, 81 and 81.0 are not the same number. So if you leave out the .0, you get a different answer. Why? The simple explanation is that 81 is a whole number, and 81.0 is a decimal. Whole number math is always rounded to the nearest whole number. Decimal math shows decimal fractions and is more accurate.

MAKE MISTAKES

If the shell can't understand what you want — either because you made a mistake or because you tried to confuse it — it complains to you with a message in red that means "I didn't understand that last command. Try again."

Python can show all kinds of error messages. When you've used Python for a while, you can see the messages are trying to give you useful hints. Until then, they're hard to understand because they look kind of random. This is a problem with most programming languages. When something goes wrong and you see error messages, they look like weird not-quite-English. They're often not as clear and helpful as they could be.

REMEMBER INFORMATION

Programming languages spend a lot of time remembering information. In most languages, including Python, you remember things by making imaginary boxes to store the information. You have to give each box a different name so that you don't get them mixed up.

Boxes hold one piece of information at a time. You can change what's in a box, and you can open the lid to see what's inside.

As a simple start, store a number in a box. In computer-speak, boxes are called *variables*. This is a big, scary word, but it just means a box for numbers.

You can store almost anything in boxes — words, music, video clips, websites, names, and addresses, but they all need more complicated code. Don't worry about how to make it work yet!

When you learn more about Python, you'll see that you can put boxes inside other boxes to make *collections*. Often, it's useful to do something to lots of boxes at the same time. It's much easier to do this if you put them in a collection. Otherwise, you end up with boxes all over the floor and a giant mess.

MAKE A VARIABLE

To make a variable and put a number inside it, type the following and then press Enter:

```
my_number = 1
```

You can maybe guess what this does: It makes a box called `my_number` and puts 1 in it.

The line between the two words in the box name is called an underscore. It's not the same as minus sign. If you type a minus sign by mistake, Python gets confused. On most keyboards, you can type an underscore by holding down the Shift key and pressing the key with the minus sign.

If you don't make any mistakes, Python swallows this code, and nothing much seems to happen. Python shows a prompt on a new line and carries on waiting.

But if you type

```
print (my_number)
```

and press Enter again, Python shows the value you told it to remember.

The print command doesn't print on paper — it prints on the screen. In the shell, you don't have to type print to look inside a box. It's included here to make the examples clearer. But if you're in a hurry, you can leave it out and just type the variable name. This works only in the shell! In the editor, you have to use print when you want Python to show you what's inside a variable.

You can make lots of boxes. As long as they all have different names, Python remembers what's inside them.

CHANGE A VARIABLE

Variables are variable, so you can change them. Type

```
my_number = 2
print (my_number)
```

and press Enter. Your box has 2 in it. (The old 1 is replaced and thrown away.)

USE VARIABLES

Why waste time putting numbers in boxes? Here's a neat magic trick: You can tell Python to do math on numbers in boxes. Type the following (and don't forget to press Enter at the end of every line):

```
my_other_number = 10
my_number*my_other_number
```

Python does its calculator thing on the numbers in the boxes.

This is HUGE! It means that when you have lots of variables and all kinds of information, you can combine everything in complicated ways.

For example, instead of adding up a list of numbers by hand, you can give them to Python, and it can do the sum for you. If any of the numbers change, you can change the value in one box and tell Python to redo the sum.

You don't have to type all the numbers again. Awesome!

MAKE RECIPES

You have gained your first computer superpowers. You can make boxes, put values in them, and do math on them. One final god-like trick is to put the value of math you do into a new box, like this:

```
my_big_number = my_number * my_other_number
```

```
Python 2.7.9 (default, Mar  8 2015, 00:52:26)
[GCC 4.9.2] on linux2
Type "copyright", "credits" or "license()" for more information.
>>> my_number = 1
>>> print (my_number)
1
>>> my_number = 2
>>> print (my_number)
2
>>> my_other_number = 154765876987
>>> my_big_number = my_number * my_other_number
>>> print (my_big_number)
309531753974
>>>
```

In computer-speak, use the * symbol when you want to multiply numbers. It's usually above the number 9 on the number pad on your keyboard or on Shift + 8. Don't use x or X because Python will think you're trying to do something with text or letters or something, and it won't work.

This one line of code is beyond awesome. You've made a *recipe* for working with information. You don't need to know what's in the boxes. The code just works as long as the variables hold numbers. It doesn't care what the numbers are. It works for *all* of them.

You can't multiply words, collections, photos, or music!

Writing a computer program often means making a list of recipes. For example, instead of doing math on specific numbers, you can make a list of math recipes. Then you can use them over and over whenever you need some math to happen.

This is why computers are so useful. You can build recipes that do useful things to almost any kind of information — not just numbers, but words, videos, music tracks, web pages, and pictures of cats being cute and dogs falling off skateboards.

In computer-speak, recipes are called *algorithms* — maybe because calling them recipes doesn't sound serious and grown-up enough. It's always better to use a difficult word when you want to look grown-up.

USE THE SHELL AND THE EDITOR

Wasn't IDLE supposed to be a code editor? How do you type and edit code in the shell? What does the shell do anyway?

In the shell window, you type code line by line directly into Python. When you press Enter, the shell checks whether your code makes sense. If it does, it sends it to Python. If Python returns a result — like the answer to a basic math problem — it shows it in the window.

In outline, the shell recipe looks like this:

1 **Show the prompt and wait for the user to type a command and press Enter.**

2 **Read in the command.**

3 **Check whether it makes sense.**

4 **If there's a problem, complain to the user and go to Step 7; if everything is fine, send the command to Python and continue to Step 5.**

5 Wait for Python to run the command and return a result.

6 If there's a result, show it in the shell window.

7 Show the prompt and wait again.

You don't need to remember this list. The point is that the shell is a computer program. The creators of Python had to sketch out a list like this so that they knew what the shell had to do. Then they wrote code for each step to make it work.

Python is really, really complicated on the inside. But when you make your own programs, it's a good idea to sketch out the steps for your code before you start.

A sketch of steps is sometimes called a *specification*. It's like a recipe for the entire program, but it doesn't include the code that makes each step work. A good specification outlines everything a program does. It even includes all the things that can go wrong, so the program is smart enough to handle mistakes made by human users.

A specification is a bit like a map you can use to find your way around the code. Each block of code does a small and simple thing. When you put all the blocks together, they do something big, complicated, and clever — like running Python, making a big website work, managing all the apps in your phone, or making sure your microwave makes popcorn without bursting into flames and burning down the house.

OPEN THE EDITOR WINDOW

What if you want to run a series of commands without having to type them one by one? You can also do this in IDLE, but you have to open the Editor window first.

To open it, choose File ⇨ New File. When you open a new Editor window, it's labeled Untitled. It's completely blank, with no prompt, and the menu options are different.

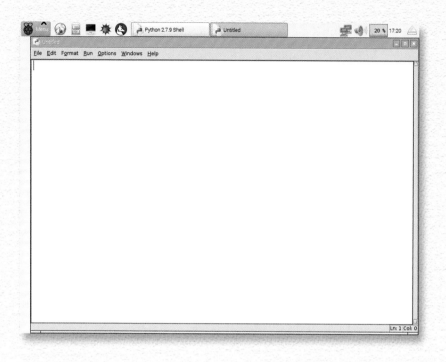

ADD CODE

To write code, type it into the window. As usual, press Enter at the end of each line. The editor doesn't try to run your code. It just moves the text cursor to the next line.

To keep things simple, type code based on the commands in the rest of this project. Make a couple of variables, put numbers in them, and do some simple math on them. Include a `print` command to show the result.

Here's some code. Remember to type it exactly as it appears here.

```
my_number = 12345
my_other_number = 56789
my_big_number = my_number * my_other_number
print (my_product)
```

When you type, the editor highlights words that Python recognizes in red. Python doesn't recognize your variables names because you invented them. It does recognize print because it's a Python command. It also highlights anything (inside brackets) so that you can check that every opening bracket has a closing bracket.

RUN CODE

How do you send the code to Python to run it? Choose Run ⇨ Run Module F5 or press F5 on your keyboard.

Aaaannd, nope, you still can't run it. That's because you have to save the code first. If you haven't saved it, Python nags you with an alert box.

Click OK in the alert box to open a Save dialog box. The file selector points to your home directory in Linux. If you logged in as the usual Pi user, this is `/home/pi`.

Type a filename and click the Save button. Python files need a `.py` extension. Remember to include it. For example, you might name the file `my_first_code.py`.

 If you're lazy you could name it a.py, but then you'll come back to your home directory a few months from now and wonder what all the Python projects you named a.py, b.py, c.py . . . do.

MAKE A PYTHON CODE FOLDER

If you want to keep all your Python projects in a folder — a good idea, but not totally essential — click Cancel in the file selector and click the File Manager icon in the top window bar. It looks like a filing cabinet.

Right-click on the file area and choose Create New ⇨ Folder. Call it `python_code`. It should be in `/home/pi`. Include the underscore and don't use a space because it makes it easier to use the directory from the Linux command line. Click the cross at the top right to close the File Manager.

 Unfortunately, you can't create directories in the file selector. This is a bad thing, but it's how it is.

MAKE A PYTHON CODE FOLDER

Now you can save the file. If you closed the Python file selector, open it again with Run ⇨ Run Module F5.

Click OK, find and double-click your new folder if you're using one, and type `my_first_code.py` in the File name box. Click Save.

Python switches to the shell window and displays a big RESTART message. If your code doesn't have any mistakes, you'll see a number like the one Python works out and displays the answer. The number you get depends on the numbers in your code and the math you did with them, because Python is doing its calculator thing, live, right in front of your eyes.

CHECK CODE

If you made a mistake, click the Editor window and look at your code again. Did you leave out an underscore or use a minus sign instead? Did you mistype the variable names so that they don't match where they should? Did you use an X instead a *? Did you add any extra letters or characters? Did you put all your code on one line?

Computers are super-picky. Python doesn't care how you spell variable names. yo_sup_dawg, bannnnnnnnnana, and ftryurgh will all work. But if you don't use *exactly* the same names throughout your code, with exactly the same spelling and underscores, Python gets very confused.

Near enough isn't good enough. Exactly means exactly the same. No exceptions. (Did I mention that already?)

LEARNING MORE PYTHON

Here are a few Python snippets that you can use to make your projects smarter.

ASK THE USER AND GET AN ANSWER

A fixed calculator is kind of useless. It's a lot more useful to get numbers and words from users and put them into boxes as the code runs so that users can do math on the numbers they want, and not on the numbers you baked into your code.

The magic code you need looks like this:

```
my_number = raw_input("Give me a number: ")
```

When you run it, Python prints "Give me a number:" and waits for the user to type something and press Enter.

It's a good idea to include a colon and a space on the end of questions. You don't have to, but it looks neater and more professional.

MAKE DECISIONS

What happens if the user types eqhguirghfrh3kj instead of a number? Nothing at all. Python carries on until it tries to multiply eqhguirghfrh3kj by sarhgfwhrj4k. Then it stops and complains that it can't do that.

You often have to include tests and make decisions in code. Making sure that you get what you need from a user can get really complicated. But the basic idea is that you include a test and skip some code if the test doesn't work out.

For example, to check whether a user typed some letters instead of a number, you can use

```
if type(my_number) == str:
    more code goes here
```

You have to put a colon at the end of a test. And you have to hit the Tab key at the start of the next line. This tells Python to run that code if the test is true, but ignore it otherwise. Stop tabbing when you get back to normal code.

The == means check whether these two things are the same. Here's a table of other tests you can use.

MORE TESTS IN PYTHON

Code	What It Means
==	Are two things the same?
!=	Are two things different?
>=	Is the first thing bigger than the second thing? (Numbers only!)
<=	Is the first thing smaller than the second thing? (Numbers only!)

Making bulletproof tests for user input turns out to be really hard. If you get it wrong, your code can stop working because Python doesn't know what to do. A good way around this is to use `try` and `except` for tests. This catches Python-stopping errors before they can stop Python. Look for examples online.

TEST TWO OR MORE THINGS AT THE SAME TIME

Often you want to check two things at once. You can combine tests with and and or, like this:

```
if something == True and something_else == False:
    more code goes here
```

If you use and, the test passes if both things are true. If you use or, the test passes if at least one thing is true. You can also use not in front of any test if you don't want it to be true.

You can use True and False in your tests. Obviously, True is always true, and False is always false. Don't forget to include the initial capital letter! true *and* false *don't work.*

REPEAT TESTS

Sometimes you want to keep doing something over and over until you decide to stop. There's more than one way to do this. Here's one example. It's called a `while` loop.

```
count = 0
while (count <= 9):
    print 'The count is: ', count
    count = count + 1
print "Okay, we're done."
```

Can you guess what this code does? It goes around and around a `while` loop adding 1 to a variable called `count`. When `count` gets to 9, the code stops counting and prints a message.

You don't have to use `while` loops for counting. You can use them for anything that needs to be done over and over until it doesn't — such as going through a word one letter at a time or checking a website over and over until something changes on it.

LEARN TO COUNT

The easy way to count is to use a `for` loop, like this:

```
for number in range(0, 10):
    print (number)
```

`range` tells Python when to start and stop counting. It doesn't include the last number, so this code counts from 0 to 9.

It's hard to remember this. It would be much more logical if it included the last number. But it doesn't.

GET THE TABS RIGHT

Loops and tests all need the tab thing and the colon. If you include a loop inside a test, or a test inside a test, or a loop inside a loop, you have to tab twice so that Python knows what to do.

```python
for x in range(0, 10):
    print (x)
    for y in range(100, 120):
        print (y)
```

You can do this more than twice, with tabbed code marching across the screen until it falls off the edge.

PULL THINGS APART

You can use `for` loops to pull things apart, like this:

```python
for letter in "Python":
    print "Current Letter is: ", letter
```

This code pulls apart the word "Python" one letter at a time, in order, and prints it on the screen.

PROJECT 6 MASTER MINECRAFT WITH PYTHON

MINECRAFT IS THE WORLD'S MOST POPULAR ONLINE BLOCK MINING GAME. (Actually it's pretty much the world's only online block mining game. It's still very popular.) Python is one of the world's most popular computer languages. How could they not go together?

GETTING STARTED WITH MINECRAFT

You can find the Pi edition of Minecraft in the Games heading of the main menu. Click the Menu button and choose Games ⇨ Minecraft Pi. Minecraft launches in a small window and asks you to start a new game or join a game.

Click Start Game, click World, and click Create New. Minecraft shows a Generating World window as it makes a new world. This takes a while. . . .

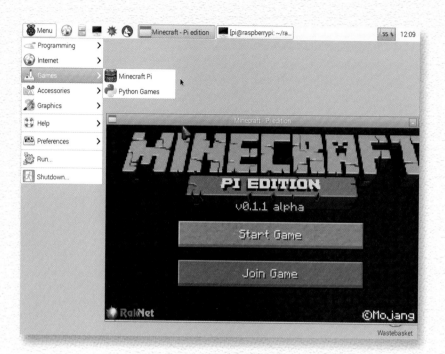

If you can't see Create New because it has fallen off the bottom of the screen, click and drag the Minecraft window upward. Minecraft is unusual. It makes a window appear, but it doesn't fit inside it. This is probably a mistake (also known as a bug).

The Pi edition of Minecraft is very simple. It doesn't have most of the features of the full version, which include hell areas, dangerous chickens, witches, ocelots, slime, and flying pigs. For more, see http://minecraft.net.

EXPLORING THE WORLD

The Minecraft world is made of blocks arranged in a 3D grid. Drag the mouse to turn so that you can see different parts of the world. To move, press the keys listed in the table.

MOVING IN MINECRAFT

Key	New Direction
W	Move forward
A	Shuffle left without turning
D	Shuffle right without turning
S	Move back
E	Show the blocks window
Esc after E	Hide the block window
Space	Jump once
Double-tap space	If not flying, start to fly If flying, stop and fall (ouch!)
Tab	Release the mouse so that you can use it on the desktop
Esc	Go the Game menu

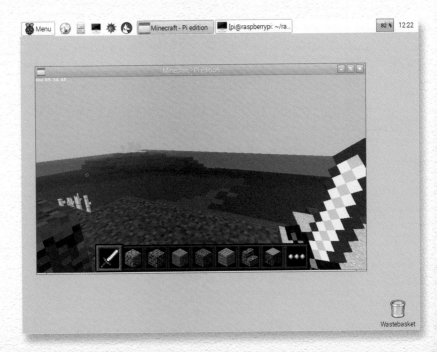

CHANGING THE VIEW

You may find it hard to use the default first-person view, which puts the camera in front of your player's eyes. It's kind of clumsy, and it's hard to see where you are.

To change the view, press Esc and click the second button at the top left of the window. When the icon changes to a rectangle with lines leading to a pair of blocks, click Back to Game.

Now the camera is behind your player. Some people prefer this view because it's easier to see what's happening.

CHANGING THE WORLD

Minecraft is all about changing your world. To remove a block, click the left mouse button to swing your sword. After you hit a block a few times, it breaks into pieces and disappears.

 It's hard to aim in Minecraft. You have to practice to work out which block your sword is going to hit.

If nothing happens when you left-click, move your player until a block is in front of you.

To build something new, press E to see all the blocks and other items you can use. Click one to select it. If it's a block and not a weapon, right-click to add it to the world. You can keep right-clicking, turning, and moving to add more and more blocks.

UNDERSTANDING APIs

In computerland, an API (Application Program Interface) is a software control panel for a website, game, or other app. Instead of clicking a mouse and pressing keys to make things happen, you can send software commands using code. APIs can also tell you what's happening inside a website, game, or app.

APIs are everywhere. Twitter, Facebook, and other big websites have their own APIs. As an example, here are a few things you can do with the Twitter API. This isn't the full list, but it does give you some hints:

» Make useful things happen automatically. For example, you can use the Twitter API to send tweets automatically at set times. You don't have to be anywhere near a computer or phone to tweet!

» Collect information. For example, you can use the API to ask Twitter once a day how many followers you have and then draw a graph of the numbers.

» Add smart new features. Do you want to follow everyone who posts a word you're interested in, like the name of a band or a hot news topic? You can use the API to make it happen.

UNDERSTANDING THE MINECRAFT API

The Minecraft API built into the Pi version is much simpler than the Twitter API. But you can still do some cool things with it. Here are some possibilities:

» Find out where your player is.

» Teleport your player to a new location.

» Build complicated shapes with blocks.

» Remove blocks with code — maybe to clear a big area.

LOOKING AT THE MINECRAFT API

All APIs have a reference website with a list of commands — also known as *API calls,* or just calls for short. The Minecraft API Reference is at www.stuffaboutcode.com/p/minecraft-api-reference.html.

API reference pages often look complicated, but usually that's because you get a list of calls and not quite enough explanation of what each call does, or how to use it, with examples.

The Minecraft API Reference has good examples, but the explanations are not very detailed. You have to do some guessing, which is normal when you're using an API.

Another common API problem is that you have no idea which calls are used a lot and which calls aren't. All the calls get equal space, so you can't tell which ones you need to learn and which ones you can ignore.

When you're learning an API, it's a good idea to look through the list and copy/paste or make a note of calls that look interesting or useful. Then you can experiment with them. And if you need to know more about them, you can look online for other examples.

Never try to learn all of an API before using it. You'd need a brain the size of a planet — which would make it hard to get out of bed in the morning — and a perfect memory. It's fine to keep looking stuff up. If you use an API a lot, you often learn the most useful calls without really trying.

USING THE MINECRAFT API

Most projects that use an API start with *boilerplate* code that sets up the API so that you can use it later. For Minecraft, the boilerplate code looks like this:

```
from mcpi import minecraft
mc = minecraft.Minecraft.create()
```

The code makes a variable called mc, which works like an invisible Minecraft control robot. When you send commands to mc, it passes them to Minecraft. Minecraft does the stuff you tell it to, or reports back with information you asked for, or both.

The API works by sending special messages to Minecraft — a bit like emails or texts. APIs are good at hiding details. They make it easy to concentrate on what you want to happen without worrying about all the incredibly complicated messaging and testing and thinking about stuff that goes on out of sight.

USING AN API CALL

Here's a simple example. Choose Menu ⇨ Programming ⇨ Python 2 to launch the Python 2 editor. Then choose File ⇨ New Window to make a new file.

Type the following code:

```
from mcpi import minecraft
mc = minecraft.Minecraft.create()
x, y, z = mc.player.getPos()
print x, y, z
```

Can you guess what this does? Save the file as wherami.py. Launch Minecraft if it's not already running. Move around inside the game for a bit.

Then click the code window in the Python editor again and press F5 to run the code.

Move the player again and run the code again. The code tells you where your player is in the Minecraft world! It uses three numbers. The table tells you what they mean.

FINDING YOURSELF IN MINECRAFT

Letter	What It Means
x	East/west on the grid
y	Up/down for flying and digging
z	North/south on the grid

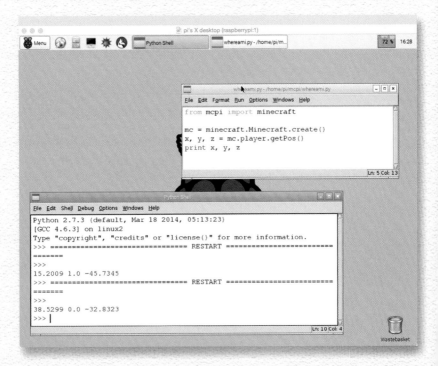

There's no big arrow pointing north in Minecraft, so x and z are just for guidance. North is always in the same direction, somewhere . . . over there. But it's not usually the direction you're facing.

TELEPORTING IN MINECRAFT

You can use a different API call to move around in Minecraft. Change the code so that it looks like this:

```
from mcpi import minecraft
mc = minecraft.Minecraft.create()
x, y, z = mc.player.getPos()
mc.player.setPos(x, y + 100, z)
```

The setPos() API call moves your player to a new location. You can do some basic math to the x, y, z numbers to move from your current location to a new one. Or you can use some other numbers — maybe random numbers — to jump to some other place.

Save the file as jump.py and press F5 to run it. The code makes you jump straight up by 100 grid blocks. If you're flying, you stay there. If you're not flying, you crash straight back down again.

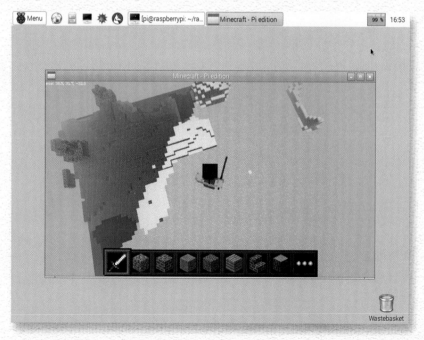

You don't die when you crash. Your player is made of very tough blocks.

REMOVING BLOCKS

Hacking away at blocks with a sword is a really slow way to change the world. Is there a faster way?

If you look through the API, you won't find a `deleteBlock()` call. But there is a `setBlock()` call. It turns a block into a different kind of block.

Can you work out how to make blocks disappear now? You have to use a trick. In Minecraft, the entire world is made of blocks — across, left, right, up and down, in every direction — so there are no missing blocks.

The trick? Empty blocks are made of air. You can use `setBlock()` to turn stone and other blocks into air blocks to make them disappear.

Here's some code:

```
from mcpi import minecraft
from time import sleep

while True:
    mc = minecraft.Minecraft.create()
    mc.setBlock(x, y - 1, z, 0)
    sleep (0.1)
```

The game is called Minecraft, so let's make a mine. The code removes the block your player is standing on. It loops forever, so it keeps removing blocks. The player falls into a bottomless shaft that gets deeper and deeper.

Save it as `death_dig.py` and run it. You may need to nudge your character into a hole to make the mineshaft appear. If you dig deep enough, Minecraft decides you've fallen out of the bottom of the earth and kills you. It would take an hour or two to get this far with just a sword.

The 0 at the end of the setBlock() call makes the block an air block. There are lots of different block types in Minecraft, and they all have a different number. If you scroll through the API Reference, you can find a list of block types, with the number of each.

MAKING BUILDINGS

Of course, you can also take an air block and turn it into a stone or water block. Try the following:

```
from mcpi import minecraft
import random
mc = minecraft.Minecraft.create()

x, y, z = mc.player.getPos()
x = x + random.randint(-10, 10)
z = z + random.randint(-10, 10)
for i in range(0, 21):
    mc.setBlock(x, y + i, z, random.randint(1, 8))
```

Can you work out what this does? The `random.randint(a, b)` calls produce a random — unpredictable — number between the first and second numbers in the brackets. For example:

```
random.randint(-10, 10)
```

makes a number between –10 and 10. You get a different number every time you run this code. It's designed to be unpredictable.

Random code is a good way to add surprises. You can give the code an outline of something, and it fills in the details in surprising ways.

Here, the x and z positions are random, so they stay close to the player (but not likely to be on top of the player).

Why does this matter? Because the rest of the code makes a simple building on the random position. It turns air blocks into other blocks.

The small 1, 8 range of randomness more or less guarantees that one of the blocks will be flowing water. Put it all together, and you get a fountain!

Minecraft makes the water pour off the fountain onto the ground and into the sea. Because the blocks are random, the fountain is a little different every time you run the code.

PROJECT 7 MORE THINGS TO SEE AND DO

THIS IS A SMALL BOOK ABOUT A BIG SUBJECT. Your Pi is like a giant toy box. When you start playing with code, the toy box gets so big you can't see the bottom or the sides, and there's always more to learn and explore. Here are some more projects you can try.

SCRATCH

You can make entire games out of Scratch scripts — and kids do. Here are some projects that lead up to a full game.

» Work out how to have two sprites moving on the stage at the same time. Once you know how to work with two sprites, you can copy the code to work with as many sprites as you want.

» Research costumes. Find out how to change the look of your sprites.

» Find out how to play sounds in Scratch. Scratch isn't as good at music as Sonic Pi is, but some of the blocks can play simple sounds and notes, and you can build scripts to play tunes.

» Find out about costume animation. See whether you can make a sprite walk by looping through a series of costumes.

» Write a script that does something when two sprites overlap. For example, you can make either or both sprites say "Ouch!" Or you can make one sprite disappear or change costume.

» Work out how to use the keyboard to move a sprite left and right. A lot of games use this idea.

» Work out how to make a sprite create a new sprite when you press a key. You can use this script to make a gun that fires shapes at another sprite.

» Make a complete game. Include scoring and sounds.

Although Scratch doesn't have chat or email, you can use the Scratch website (https://scratch.mit.edu) to share games and other Scratch projects and to look at the code other kids have created.

Some of the games are really clever. But because you can look at the code in Scratch, you can see how the games were put together and learn some cool new tricks. Don't forget to check out the Best Games page at https://scratch.mit.edu/studios/26995.

SONIC PI

You don't have to know a lot about music to have fun with Sonic Pi. It helps, but it's not essential. Try the following:

» Make Sonic Pi play a simple tune. Maybe try something simple like "Twinkle Twinkle Little Star" or "Three Blind Mice." If you can't read music at all, try making a song by ear, matching the notes from a recording or video — try YouTube — to your Sonic Pi code.

» Explore different ways to make notes, lists of notes, and repeating sections. You can usually find more than one way to do things in Sonic Pi.

» Try all the synthesizer sounds. There are a lot of sounds to choose from, and they all sound different. How would you use them in a bigger track?

» Learn about Sonic Pi samples. Sonic Pi includes a big collection of built-in sounds, called samples. How are they different from synthesizer sounds? What happens if you play them with different settings?

» Learn about Sonic Pi Effects. Effects transform sounds in all kinds of ways. Some effects, like echo, are easy to understand. Others are more complicated. Try playing with them and thinking about how you can use them. Have you heard the same effects on your favorite music?

Sonic Pi is good for live coding, where you can make music as you type. But it's also good for writing code that writes music. This is called *generative music,* which just means that Sonic Pi is writing the music for you. Instead of typing in long lists of notes, the Pi uses random numbers and maybe some rules to compose the music — and it's different every time you run the code.

PYTHON PROJECTS

You could literally spend five years learning Python, and you still wouldn't know everything there is to know about it.

» Learn how to repeat code with functions. Code is often made of sections that solve a problem or do something useful. You usually kick the useful code into a separate block called a function so that you can use it over and over without having to retype it every time. Look up Python functions online and see whether you can write some code that uses them.

» Make a simple guessing game. Write some code that thinks of a number between 1 and 10 and tells you whether you guessed it right. Then try to write some code that guesses a number you made up. What's the fastest way to guess the number? Is there a better way than trying all the numbers one after the other in order?

» Make shapes with Turtle Graphics. Python includes a simple drawing robot called a turtle. You can use very simple turtle code to make very complicated shapes, especially when you combine the graphics with functions. Find out how to use Turtle Graphics on the Pi and then see what kind of cool shapes you can make. Try finding some shapes online and copying them.

» Explore Pygame. Pygame is a collection of Python code you can glue together to make your own games. Using Pygame is much easier than writing everything you need on your own. You can't make a world-beating first-person shooter with Pygame — it's not fast enough — but it's good enough for simple arcade games. It's also a good next step when you outgrow Scratch. For more, see the Pygame site at http://pygame.org.

» Use Python to copy or move some files from one folder to another. You'll have to learn a lot about how the Linux file system works before you can do this one. The code doesn't have to be complicated, but working out how to make Python work with Linux and how to do clever things with files is probably harder than you're expecting!

MINECRAFT AND PYTHON

Some of these projects are harder than others. A few are very hard, but see how far you get with them anyway. You'll have to research more about Python to make some of them work.

» Remove blocks as you walk. This one is harder than it looks. How many layers of blocks do you need to get rid of before you can walk through the hole you make? How wide does the hole need to be? The easy option is to use lots of separate calls to `setBlock()`. Is there a neater way to make the code work with loops or conditionals?

» Build bigger shapes. Cubes and blocks of blocks are easy. There's a special API call for big square shapes with lots of blocks. But how about making a square, or a pyramid, or a grid of lines? If you know a lot about math, you can try making circles or spheres. If you don't, try building a house.

» Build a rocket. Take the fountain/tower and make it fly into the sky. How do you keep the blocks together? Is there a simpler way to do it?

» Make a firework. At a certain height — say 100 blocks — make all the blocks in the rocket explode in different directions. How can you keep track of the position of every block?

DEDICATION

Dedicated to Team HGA. (*Scientia potestas est.*)

ABOUT THE AUTHOR

Richard Wentk has been building useful things out of words, electronic parts, code, and the Internet for more than 35 years. He is a regular contributor to various UK technology magazines and is the author of *Teach Yourself Visually Raspberry Pi, iOS App Development Portable Genius,* and more than ten other titles. He lives on the South Coast of England surrounded by beaches, gardens, high-speed broadband, and an unusually large collection of Raspberry Pis.

AUTHOR'S ACKNOWLEDGMENTS

Books are always a team effort. I'd like to thank Katie Mohr for getting the project started and to Kelly Ewing for shepherding it to a successful conclusion.

Of course, the book wouldn't have been possible without the efforts of the Raspberry Pi Foundation to bring affordable computing to a new generation and to the thousands of developers who contribute their time and expertise for free in the Open Source community to make projects like the Pi possible. They also deserve many thanks.

PUBLISHER'S ACKNOWLEDGMENTS

Senior Acquisitions Editor: Katie Mohr

Project Editor: Kelly Ewing

Copy Editor: Kelly Ewing

Editorial Assistant: Matthew Lowe

Sr. Editorial Assistant: Cherie Case

Production Editor: Vasanth Koilraj

Cover Image: ©Wiley